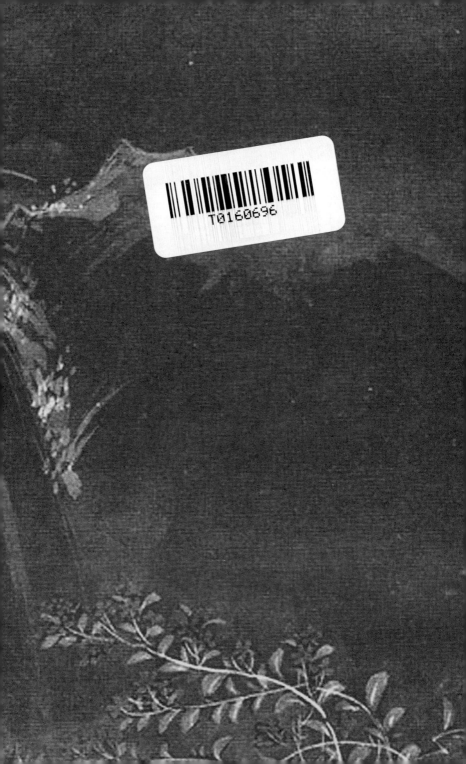

ZEN
MASTERS
OF
JAPAN

RICHARD BRYAN McDANIEL

ZEN MASTERS OF JAPAN

THE SECOND STEP EAST

TUTTLE Publishing

Tokyo | Rutland, Vermont | Singapore

Published by Tuttle Publishing, an imprint of Periplus Editions (HK) Ltd.

www.tuttlepublishing.com

Copyright © 2013 Richard Bryan McDaniel

Library of Congress Cataloging-in-Publication Data in Process

ISBN 978-4-8053-1272-8

Distributed by

North America, Latin America & Europe
Tuttle Publishing
364 Innovation Drive
North Clarendon
VT 05759-9436 U.S.A.
Tel: 1 (802) 773-8930
Fax: 1 (802) 773-6993
info@tuttlepublishing.com
www.tuttlepublishing.com

Japan
Tuttle Publishing
Yaekari Building 3rd Floor
5-4-12 Osaki, Shinagawa-ku
Tokyo 1410032, Japan
Tel: (81) 3 5437 0171
Fax: (81) 3 5437 0755
sales@tuttle.co.jp
www.tuttle.co.jp

Asia Pacific
Berkeley Books Pte. Ltd.
61 Tai Seng Avenue #02-12
Singapore 534167
Tel: (65) 6280-1330
Fax: (65) 6280-6290
inquiries@periplus.com.sg
www.periplus.com

First edition
17 16 15 14 13   10 9 8 7 6 5 4 3 2 1   1307RP
Printed in China

Front jacket illustration: Portrait of Bodhidharma and Huike by Sesshu Toyo
Author photograph courtesy of Geoffrey Gammon

Contents

List of Illustrations 7
Preface 9
Prologue in China 17

CHAPTER ONE
The Pioneers 27
Kakua 28
Myoan Eisai 36
Ryonen Myozen 42

CHAPTER TWO
Dogen Kigen 45

CHAPTER THREE
Dogen's Successors 61
Koun Ejo 63
Tettsu Gikai 67
Gien 70

CHAPTER FOUR
Chinese Connections 73
Bukko Kokushi 74
Chiyono [Mugai Nyodai] .. 77
Enni Ben'en [Shoichi
Kokushi] 79
Mukan Fumon [Daimin
Kokushi] 82

Shinchi Kakushin 83
Nampo Jomyo [Daio
Kokushi] 85

CHAPTER FIVE
Hanazono's Zen Masters 89
Shuho Myocho [Daito
Kokushi] 90
Kanzan Egen 97

CHAPTER SIX
Temple Founders 101
Keizan Jokin 102
Muso Soseki 107

CHAPTER SEVEN
Bassui 115

CHAPTER EIGHT
Ikkyu Sojun 127

CHAPTER NINE
Zen Style 143
Sesshu Toyo 147
Murata Shuko 149
Soeki Rikyu 151

CHAPTER TEN

Takuan Soho and Martial Zen..................... 157

CHAPTER ELEVEN

Suzuki Shosan 169

CHAPTER TWELVE

Four 17ᵗʰ Century Masters. 183
Gudo Toshoku.................. 184
Shido Munan.................... 186
Ingen Ryuki..................... 190
Dokutan Shokei............... 192

CHAPTER THIRTEEN

Bankei Yotaku.................. 195

CHAPTER FOURTEEN

The Poet........................... 211
Matsuo Basho.................. 212
Joso.................................. 221

CHAPTER FIFTEEN

Shoju Rojin and His Disciple.................... 225
Dokyo Etan
[Shoju Rojin].................... 226
Hakuin Ekaku
[beginning]....................... 229

CHAPTER SIXTEEN

Hakuin Ekaku 237

CHAPTER SEVENTEEN

Hakuin's Heirs................. 253
Torei Enji......................... 254
Gasan Jito........................ 260
Inzan Ien.......................... 262
Takuju Kosen.................... 264

CHAPTER EIGHTEEN

Sengai Gibon and Ryokan Daigu................. 267
Sengai Gibon.................... 268
Ryokan Daigu.................. 276

CHAPTER NINETEEN

The Meiji Era................. 287
Nan-in.............................. 292
Tanzan............................. 292
Ogino Dokuon.................. 293
Imakita Kosen.................. 294
Soyen Shaku 295

Epilogue in Chicago.......... 301
Acknowledgments.............. 303
Notes 305
Bibliography 309
Index of Stories.................. 313

List of Illustrations

Prologue: Portrait of Bodhidharma and Huike by Sesshu Toyo 16

Chapter One: Landscape by Sesshu Toyo 26

Chapter Two: Portrait of Dogen 44

Chapter Three: "Circle, Triangle, Square" by Sengai Gibon ... 60

Chapter Four: Zen-style landscape painting by
Tani Buncho (1763-1840) 72

Chapter Five: Portrait of "Gold Coin Ebisu" by Sengai Gibon . 88

Chapter Six: Portrait of Muso Soseki 100

Chapter Seven: "Hotei Awakes" by Sengai Gibon 114

Chapter Eight: Portrait of Ikkyu Sojun................................. 126

Chapter Nine: Ink splash painting by Sesshu Toyo.............. 142

Chapter Ten: Portrait of Soeki Rikyu.................................... 156

Chapter Eleven: Portrait of Bodhidharma by Hakuin Ekaku.. 168

Chapter Twelve: Portrait of Ingen Ryuki 182

Chapter Thirteen: Landscape by Sesshu Toyo....................... 194

Chapter Fourteen: Portrait of Matsuo Basho 210

Chapter Fifteen: Painting and haiku by Matsuo Basho......... 224

Chapter Sixteen: Self portrait by Hakuin Ekaku................... 236

Chapter Seventeen: "Kanzan and Jittoku" by Sengai Gibon ... 252

Chapter Eighteen: "Tea Implements" by Sengai Gibon 266

Chapter Nineteen: Portait of Soyen Shaku by
Molly Macnaughton 286

Preface

This is the second of three volumes in which I gather together the Zen stories of China, Japan, and North America. As I explained in the Preface to *Zen Masters of China: The First Step East*, it was these stories that originally intrigued me and drew me to the practice of Zen.

Consider, for example, this brief Chinese tale:

A new student came to work with the 9th century Chinese master, Zhaozhou Congshen. He presented himself, saying, "I have just entered the monastery, and I beg you to accept me as a disciple and teach me."

Zhaozhou asked him, "Have you had anything to eat yet?"

"Yes, I have. Thank you."

"Then you had better wash your bowl," Zhaozhou told him. And we are informed that upon hearing these words, the new monk attained enlightenment or awakening.

There is a comparable Japanese tale of a nun, named Chiyono, who came to awakening when the bottom broke from the pail she was carrying, and the moon was no longer reflected in the water.

The obscurity of these stories, when I first encountered them, was what made them so compelling. They were unlike anything with which I was familiar in the realm of religious literature. The stories made no reference to a deity or to morality. There were no miraculous events. Indeed, the events described—washing bowls, pails breaking—were of the most commonplace sort.

I pointed out in that earlier Preface that the

—lore of religion begins in myth, passes through legend, and only slowly comes to verifiable historical narrative. One sees this pattern in the dominant religious traditions of the West. First there are the tales of the Bible, followed by the legends of Christian saints and Jewish folklore. And only in the later centuries do we have what might be considered objectively accurate information.

The stories of Zen likewise begin with the anecdotes of 6th century China, pass through the legends of the Tang and Song Dynasties as well as of Japan, and continue in the records of the Zen teachers of more recent centuries, including those pioneers who brought the tradition to the world outside of Asia.

The spread of the teaching has been steadily eastward. From China, various schools of Buddhism, including Chan, spread to Korea, Vietnam, and Japan (where it was called Zen). While over time the Chan School declined in China, it continued to flourish in Japan where it had its fullest flowering. Finally, at the end of the 19th century, Zen took its longest stride east, across the Pacific Ocean to the shores of North America. (1)

The format of this volume differs in some significant ways from that of the first. To begin with, the time frame considered is much broader, and consequently I have made no attempt to be as inclusive as I was in the book on China. Instead, I focus on a select group of Zen Masters who are recognized for the impact they had on the development of the tradition in Japan. There may well have been other masters and students whose spiritual attainments equaled or surpassed those of the individuals I include in this collection, but these are the figures whose lives, for one reason or another, achieved legendary status.

Because there is more biographical information available about these masters, we have a clearer understanding of them as individuals than we do of their Chinese predecessors. As figures of legend, however, they were also often the subjects of popular tales based more in folklore than in fact. Those apocryphal tales are included in this volume because, while they may have limited historical value, they have become part of an unofficial Zen canon—part of what I have called the "folk history" of Zen. For example, we not only have Hakuin's autobiographical and instructional writings, we also have several records written by his students. In addition to those, there are a number of tales such as the story about the young girl who accused Hakuin of being the father of her child. While it is unlikely that these stories are based in actual events, they have become part of the folk history.

Because Zen came to permeate the cultural spirit of Japan in a way it did not do in China, more attention is paid to the setting and historical context of the tales than was paid to those in my first book.

As with that first volume, there is no new material in this collection. All the stories gathered here have been told in English elsewhere. And once more I have retained the story-teller's prerogative of making minor embellishments.

In the first book, it was necessary to decide which of three possible renderings I would give of Chinese names. In this volume, I have chosen to use the Japanese forms of those names throughout, even in the Prologue. Where appropriate I provide the Pinyin Romanization in brackets.

Finally, I point out once again that Zen is, above all, a practice. There is more information about the practice of zazen in this book than there was in the first, but this still is not a book of instruction. For those readers interested in the actual practice of Zen, I recommend either Albert Low's *Zen Meditation: Plain and Simple* [originally published as *An Invitation to Practice Zen*] or Robert Aitkin's *Taking the Path of Zen*.

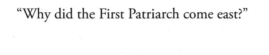

"Why did the First Patriarch come east?"

ZEN
MASTERS
OF
JAPAN

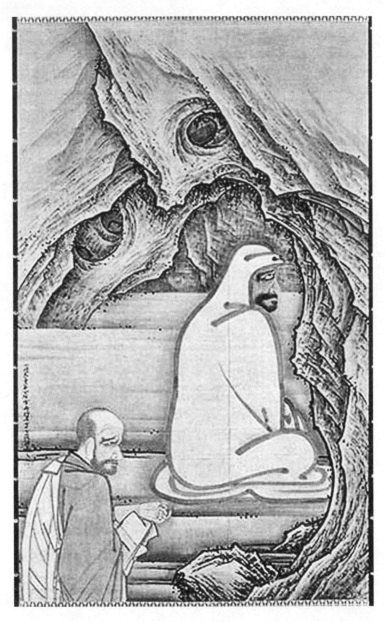

Portrait of Bodhidharma and Huike by Sesshu Toyo

Prologue in China

"Zen" is the Japanese pronunciation of the Chinese character "chan," which, in turn, was the Chinese rendering of the Sanskrit word "dhyana," usually translated into English as "meditation." The etymology of the word reflects the steady eastward movement of the meditation school of Buddhism from India to China, thence to Japan, and eventually beyond Asia.

Legend has it that Zen was brought to China by an Indian monk named Bodhidharma, who was the 28th Patriarch—or "ancestor"—of the meditation school in that region. The first Patriarch had been the Buddha himself.

"Buddha" is not a name, but rather a title. It usually, but not always, refers to Siddhartha Gautama also known as Sakyamuni, the Sage of the Sakya Clan. The title means the "awakened" or "enlightened" one. Gautama attained awakening by meditation, and as a result, came to realize that his fundamental nature was no different from that of all existence. The teachings of Sakyamuni were originally intended to help other persons attain the same awakening, to become, like him, a "buddha."

Bodhidharma began studying with his own teacher, the 27th Patriarch, Prajanatara, one thousand years after the death of the Buddha. Over time the Buddhist tradition had split into two major branches: the conservative Theravada (the Teaching of the Elders) which spread to Sri Lanka and Southeast Asia, and the more liberal, but also at times more fanciful, Mahayana which spread north to Tibet, China, and Korea. It was out of the Mahayana tradition (and partially in reaction to it) that Zen would evolve.

By the time of Prajanatara and Bodhidharma, the Mahayana had also broken into a number of competing schools, many of which were speculative and abstract. Monks spent as much or more time analyzing the scriptures, known as sutras, as in meditating. Their faith had become theoretical rather than grounded in the experience of awakening that the Buddha had advocated, the experience the Japanese would later term *kensho* [*ken*, seeing into or understanding something; *sho*, one's true nature].

Saddened by the deteriorated condition of Buddhism in India, Prajanatara suggested that Bodhidharma travel to China to determine if that land was a suitable environment in which to revitalize the meditation school which still sought to foster the experience of awakening in its practitioners. As a result of that journey, Bodhidharma is considered the First Patriarch of Chinese Zen.

Buddhism was already well established in the "Celestial Kingdom" when Bodhidharma arrived there, and Chinese Buddhists, as well as Daoists and Confucionists, would come to wonder how his teaching differed from that of other Buddhist sects. One of the formal ways in which that question was posed was to ask a Zen teacher, "Why did the First Patriarch come east?" What did Bodhidharma bring that had not already come to China?

The story of Bodhidharma's arrival in China is recounted in the first koan in a collection known as the *Blue Cliff Record* [J: *Hekiganroku*]. A koan is usually an apparently nonsensical question based on an anecdote from the lives of the Zen masters of the past—primarily those in China. The question becomes the focus of a Zen student's meditative practice and helps the student attain insight. While koans cannot be resolved through reasoning, an understanding of them can be achieved through intuition.

The story recounted in the *Blue Cliff Record* portrays Bodhidharma as a barbarian—both in the original meaning of the term (someone from elsewhere) and in the figurative sense. In the koan, Bodhidharma was given an audience with the Emperor of China, Wu Liang. The Emperor was a practicing Buddhist and proud of the many ways he had supported the tradition in his realm. When he learned that there was a visitor in his kingdom from the land where the Buddha had lived, he naturally invited Bodhidharma to come to the court. There, Wu described all he had done to promote Buddhism and asked, "What is your opinion? What merit have I accumulated as a result of these deeds?"

Bodhidharma's reply was blunt and tactless: "No merit whatsoever."

"Why not?" the Emperor demanded.

"Motives for such actions are always impure," Bodhidharma told him. "They are undertaken solely for the purposes of attaining future rebirth. They are like shadows cast by bodies, following those bodies but having no reality of their own."

"Then what is true merit?" the Emperor asked.

"It is clear seeing, pure knowing, beyond the discriminating intelligence. Its essence is emptiness. Such merit cannot be gained by worldly means."

This was unlike any exposition of the Buddhist faith the Emperor had heard before, and, perhaps a little testily, he asked, "According to your understanding, then, what is the first principle of Buddhism?"

"Vast emptiness and not a thing that can be called holy," Bodhidharma responded at once.

Wu spluttered: "What is that supposed to mean? And who are you who now stands before me?"

To which Bodhidharma replied: "I don't know." Then he left the court.

After leaving Wu Liang's court, Bodhidharma took up residence in the Shaolin temple located on Mount Songshan. There he built a hermitage on the peak of Mount Shaoshi, where he practiced silent meditation while facing the wall of a cliff which rose in front of his hut. He came to be known locally as *Biguan*, the wall-gazing Brahmin, and the hut was known as the "Wall-gazing Hermitage."

Unlike the largely academic Buddhism then common in China, Bodhidharma's practice was grounded in seated meditation, *zazen* in Japanese [*za* to sit; *zen* meditation]. He described his Buddhism as:

> A special transmission outside the scriptures;
> Not dependent on words or letters;
> By direct pointing to the mind of man,
> Seeing into one's true nature and attaining Buddhahood.

It was not a practice that had much immediate appeal to the Chinese.

There was, however, a Confucian scholar named Ji who had been searching for a teacher to help him resolve the concerns that weighed heavily on his mind. He had visited Confucian, Daoist, and Buddhist teachers and was well versed not only in the Confucian classics but also in the doctrines of both the Theravada and Mahayana traditions. Nothing, however, had brought him peace of mind. In desperation, he came to the Wall-gazing Hermitage, seeking the barbarian monk who had come from the land of the Buddha.

When Ji presented himself at Bodhidharma's hermitage, the old Indian monk suspected his visitor was another who came seeking an intellectual explanation of Buddhist doctrine rather than the experiential insight that comes from the practice of meditation. So, for a long time, he ignored Ji. The Confucian, however, remained patiently outside the hut, waiting for Bodhidharma to acknowledge him. One night, it began to snow. The snow fell so heavily that by morning, it was up to the supplicant's knees. Seeing this, Bodhidharma finally spoke, asking, "What is it you seek?"

"Your teaching," Ji told him.

"The teaching of the Buddha is subtle and difficult. Understanding can only be acquired through strenuous effort, doing what is hard to do and enduring what is hard to endure, continuing the practice for even countless eons of time. How can a man of scant virtue and great vanity, such as yourself, achieve it? Your puny efforts will only end in failure."

Ji drew his sword, cut off his left arm, and presented it to Bodhidharma as evidence of the sincerity of his intention.

"What you seek," Bodhidharma told him, "can't be found through another."

"My mind isn't at peace," Ji lamented. "Please, master, help me pacify it."

"Very well. Bring your mind here, and I'll pacify it."

"I've sought it for these many years, even practicing sitting mediation as you do, but still I'm not able to get hold of it."

"There! Now it's pacified!"

Upon hearing those words, Ji achieved awakening, the same insight that earned Gautama the title "Buddha."

After Ji's awakening, Bodhidharma gave him the name Huike, which means, "his understanding will do." By bestowing his disciple with a new name, Bodhidharma signaled his approval of the younger man's insight. This began a tradition by which a teacher recognized those students whose insight were equal to or surpassed his own and thus were worthy to be called Masters of Meditation, or Zen Masters. In the Rinzai School, the process is known as *inka* or transmission. In bestowing *inka*, the teacher acknowledges the student as his successor.

The Japanese, who developed their own pronunciation of the kanji characters they adopted from China, pronounced Huike as

"Eka." From this point forward, the Japanese renderings of Chinese names will be used.

Bodhidharma was an Indian and his understanding of both Zen and Buddhism were the product of the culture from which he came. With Eka, the slow process of developing a Chinese meditation school began. It has been suggested that Zen is the result of the coming together of the philosophical Indian Buddhist tradition with native Chinese Daoism, with its emphasis on the rhythms of nature—the natural flow, or "way" (Dao), of things.

Eka met the man to whom he would give transmission when a layman, named Sosan, who was afflicted with leprosy, approached him. The leper hoped that Eka could free him of the sins that he believed were the cause of his condition. Echoing his own teacher, Eka told Sosan, "Bring your sins here, and I'll rid you of them."

"When I reflect on my sins," the man admitted, "I'm not sure what they are."

"Then you're cleansed," Eka told him. "Now all that remains is for you to take refuge in the Buddha, the Dharma, and the Sangha." "Dharma" is the Sanskrit term for both the teachings of the Buddha and the way things are in general (the truth). "Sangha" was originally the term for the congregation of Buddhist monks and nuns.

Sosan said, "I understand that you are member of a group referred to as the Sangha, but what are the Buddha and the Dharma?"

"Mind is Buddha. Mind is Dharma. Dharma and Buddha are not two. So it is with the Sangha."

Sosan then made one of those intuitive leaps of understanding only possible when one has been considering a problem, as he had been considering the problem of sin, for a long time: "Now I understand that sins are neither within nor without," he exclaimed. "Just as the Mind is, so is Buddha, so is Dharma. They aren't two."

Eka recognized the leper as his successor and gave him the name Kanchi, which means, "jewel monk."

Sosan Kanchi would later write the *Inscription on the Believing Mind*, a verse composition that would come to be revered in Japan as well as China and is still popular with Zen practitioners today. The opening verses demonstrate the way in which Kanchi's Zen combines Daoist terminology with Buddhist principles.

> The Perfect Way [Dao] knows no difficulties
> Except that it refuses to make preference:
> Only when freed from hate and love,
> It reveals itself fully and without disguise.
>
> A tenth of an inch's difference,
> And heaven and earth are set apart;
> If you want to see it manifest,
> Take no thought either for or against it.
>
> To set up what you like against what you dislike—
> This is the disease of the mind:
> When the deep meaning of Tao is not understood
> Peace of mind is disturbed and nothing is gained. (2)

Both Eka and Sosan Kanchi dwelt in obscurity in the mountains alongside the Yangtze River because the political environment in China after the death of Emperor Wu was hostile to Buddhism. Wu's successors were traditional Confucianists who considered both Daoism (which had originated in China) and Buddhism (which they dismissed as a foreign teaching) to be disruptive elements in society. In particular, the celibate life of monks and nuns in Buddhist monasteries was repugnant to Confucianists, who put great value on family life and social responsibility. They argued that the monks and nuns living in temples such as Shaolin were parasites who contributed nothing to society.

An edict was passed banning these two traditions. Religious texts and works of art were destroyed. Monks and nuns, such as those formerly supported by the Emperor Wu, were ordered to return to lay life.

When acknowledging Sosan as his successor, Eka told him he had a responsibility to protect the teaching he had received. Therefore, instead of dwelling in the cities and towns where he would draw the attention of the authorities, he should remain in the mountains. Thus began the tradition of establishing Zen temples in mountain settings far from the activities of city life.

Regardless of how reclusive Zen masters were, highly motivated students continued to search them out. So it was that a seeker named Doshin tracked down Sosan. The third patriarch asked his visitor what he was looking for, and Doshin replied: "Please show me the way to achieve liberation."

"Who is it that holds you in bondage?" Sosan asked.

"Well, no one," Doshin admitted.

"Then why are you seeking liberation?"

These words startled the young man, and he became Sosan's disciple. After many years, he too attained awakening, and Sosan declared him his successor, giving him the robe and bowl that had been passed down from Bodhidharma.

By the time of Doshin, the suppression of Buddhism had abated and monasteries were once again open, and a formal tradition of Zen training started to evolve. Doshin instructed his disciples to be earnest in their practice of zazen. "Zazen is basic to all else. Don't bother reading the sutras; don't become involved in discussions. If you can refrain from doing so and concentrate instead on zazen, for as much as thirty-five years or more, you will benefit. Just as a monkey will eat a nut still in its shell although it's only satisfied when it has patiently extracted the nut from that shell, so there are only a few who will bring their zazen to fulfillment."

Zazen was brought to fulfillment in the "emptiness" of which Bodhidharma had spoken to Emperor Wu. But Doshin warned, "When those who are still young in the practice see emptiness, this is seeing emptiness, but it isn't real emptiness. To those who are mature in the practice and who have attained emptiness, they see neither emptiness nor non-emptiness."

The Zen school was still relatively young when Doshin taught, but it was beginning to draw seekers not only from China but from the Korean peninsula as well. One of the students who sought out Doshin came from even further away, from the islands northeast of Korea that the Chinese dismissively referred to as the Land of Wa—"the land of dwarves." (In Japanese, on the other hand, the "Land of Wa" means the "Land of Harmony.") His name was Dosho, and he is the first Japanese recorded to have studied Zen.

Dosho came to China in 653 to study with teachers of the Hosso School of Buddhism. The Hosso School is derived from an Indian tradition known as Yogacara or "Mind Only School." Its central tenet is that the world we perceive as real is only a product of mind. For a period, the Hosso School would be the primary form of Buddhism in Japan.

Dosho also became familiar with Doshin's meditation school, and when he returned to Japan he opened the first meditation hall in that country, in Nara, the city that would become the capital of Japan for much of the 8th century.

With this, Zen had taken its second step east.

Landscape by Sesshu Toyo

CHAPTER ONE

THE PIONEERS

KAKUA

MYOAN EISAI

RYONEN MYOZEN

Kakua

The earliest event to become the subject of a Zen story in Japan concerns a monk named Kakua, who made the difficult journey to China around 1172 in order to study Zen. Since Dosho had brought back the Hosso teachings, several forms of Buddhism had been established in Japan; however, the teachings of Zen (Chan) were still only to be found in the remote mountain regions of China.

After completing his training, Kakua returned to Japan. He was a recluse by nature and made no attempt to gather students. Following the example of the Zen masters of China, he lived in seclusion in the mountains of his homeland. Although he sought anonymity, stories began to circulate about him, and occasionally students would discover where he lived. They came to ask questions about what he had learned in China. Kakua would reply to their inquiries, then move further into the wilderness.

Eventually the Emperor of Japan heard about this elusive monk who had undergone numerous hardships in order to study Zen in China. Curious about how this school differed from the other branches of Buddhism with which he was familiar, the Emperor ordered Kakua to the capital to explain what wisdom he had acquired from the study of Zen. Standing before the emperor and his retinue, Kakua brought out a flute from the sleeve of his robe, blew a single note on it, then bowed and left the court.

Japan's first encounter with Buddhism had occurred in 552, when a diplomatic delegation from King Song Myong of Korea paid a visit to the court of Emperor Kimmei. The Japanese court would have been a shabby affair judged by the standards of the royal residences of China and Korea. Conditions in Japan at that time were primitive compared with those of the great Asian powers to their west. Isolated from the mainland of Asia, Japan had been protected from invasion and conquest, but for a long while it was also cut off from contact with the technological and social advances that were occurring elsewhere. The Japanese had no written language. The first steps were just then being taken to establish a central government that would be able to exert control over the various clans and tribes who, lacking other enemies, continuously warred with one another. One clan, the Yamato, argued its right to rule the entire archipelago by virtue of its claim to be descended from the first Emperor of Japan, Jimmu, and the Sun Goddess, Amaterasu. Other clans challenged this assertion and sought ways to align themselves with the divinely descended emperor through both martial and marital alliances.

There was no organized religion on the islands. There was a folk tradition that honored the spirits (*kami*) associated with certain sacred places or times of year, and there was a tradition of venerating ancestors, whose ghosts needed to be propitiated. But there was no official priesthood commissioned to conduct services; it was the responsibility of individuals or families to provide the appropriate offerings. Householders maintained a family shrine, the clan or tribe a collective shrine, and there was a national shrine in honor of the imperial household. There was no organized philosophical or moral code associated with these traditions. And it was not until these native practices were challenged by the arrival of foreign traditions that this collection of practices evolved into *Kannaga-no-michi*, or Shinto, "The Way of the Gods."

The Korean delegation of 552 brought with them a number of gifts including a statue of the Buddha and copies of several Buddhist sutras. After this meeting, certain factions in Japan, impressed by the sophistication of the Korean visitors, came to believe it was important to cultivate relationships with other nations; other factions sought to preserve national purity and unity through isolationism.

The progressives were in the ascendency during the reign of Empress Suiko (592-628), whose regent, Prince Shotoku, both modernized Japan and established the Buddhist faith on the islands. Shotoku was a great admirer of Chinese Tang dynasty culture, and he arranged for a number of expeditions to that country. Courtiers, scholars, craftsmen, and monks (like Dosho) made the hazardous crossing to the mainland and brought back with them Chinese ideas which the Japanese were able to assimilate and modify in their unique fashion. The forms of Buddhism these visitors encountered were those popular in the larger port cities on the Chinese coast; there was no contact at this point with the remote Zen communities still hidden in the mountains of China.

Using Chinese models, Shotoku worked aggressively to reform Japanese institutions, governance, the legal system, the calendar, and other branches of learning. The Chinese mode of writing, *kanji*, was adopted, with the result that while a particular character would have the same meaning in both languages, the word it represented, the sound, could be entirely different. For example, it has already been mentioned that the Japanese pronounced the characters for "Huike" as "Eka." Over time a second and more practical writing system arose, *hiragana*, based on symbols that designated syllables rather than individual sounds (letters).

Shotoku established a government bureaucracy based on Chinese models and promoted a central government in which local barons owed allegiance to the divinely descended emperor. In addition to Buddhism, Shotoku also promoted Confucianism, which he considered an appropriate vehicle for instilling in youth the virtues of loyalty, self-restraint, and commitment to duty.

Today, Shotoku is recognized as the "father of Japanese Buddhism." He composed a commentary on the Lotus Sutra, and, like the Chinese Emperor Wu, he sponsored Buddhist monasteries and temples. In popular devotional Buddhism, Shotoku is believed to be an incarnation of the Buddha; legend has it that he had been born holding a holy relic in his hand.

The new religion was not universally popular, and when the 8th century Emperor Shomu, inspired by reports of massive statues of the Buddha in China, sought to erect an even more impressive Dai Butsu (Great Buddha) in Nara, the scale of the project disturbed many who viewed Buddhism as a foreign belief system. The adherents of Shinto warned that such a statue would be an insult to the native gods of Japan. In response, Monk Gyoki of the Hosso sect, made a pilgrimage to the shrine of the Goddess Amaterasu and asked the oracles there to consult the goddess about her feelings regarding the proposed monument. The oracle recognized the Buddha as Amaterasu's emissary and declared the goddess's approval of the project.

The great bronze Buddha, not completed until after Shomu died, was 53 feet (16 meters) tall, well shy of the 85 foot (25 meter) Chinese statue; however, the hall housing the Japanese copy was enormous—284 x 166 x 152 feet (86 x 50 x 46 meters)—making it then the largest wooden structure in the world.

The controversy over the statue was representative of the tension that was developing between traditionalists, who followed the way of Shinto, and the advocates of progress and change who tended to be, at least nominally, Buddhist. Shinto strove to establish itself as the official Japanese way of devotion; the emperor was, after all, the descendant of the Shinto sun goddess. The lower classes, however, made little distinction between the two belief systems, and Shinto and Buddhist figures were often found placed side by side in popular shrines.

By the start of the second millennium, Japanese culture, wealth, and technology had become the equal of her Asian neighbors. Politically, however, the country remained in disarray. The power of the Divine Emperor waned as the power of the military leaders known as Shoguns waxed. Feudal clans—powerful families like the Fujiwara, the Minamoto, and the Sugawara—raised armies to battle one another for control of the imperial court. Even Buddhist monasteries raised armies and fought with one another. Local warlords (Daimyo) arose whose power rested in the fealty of the new warrior class of knights known as *samurai*. The warlords financed their armies by taxing the lower classes, which chose to pay taxes to them rather than to the imperial court because it was the local lords who were able to provide them some degree of protection.

Conditions reached their nadir in 1050, which began

—the Age of Degenerate Law, a dark epoch of epidemic, earthquake, fire, famine, banditry, and murder. The Fujiwara, to whom the imperial government had long since ceded its prestige, had been infected by their own decadence even as they attained the summit of their power. Their armed monks were now a threat to their own masters, and the soldiery of feudal lords in the outlying provinces was finally called upon to bring the anarchy under control. These lords—descendants of outcast emperors—detested the decadent despotism at Kyoto. Over the course of the next century, the Fujiwara were challenged and defeated by the strong provincial clans, notably the Taira or Heike, descendants of that Emperor Kwammu who had done so much to bring the Fujiwara into power. Other claimants challenged the Heike, in their turn, notably an alliance of strong clans that was grouped around the family Minamoto. In five bloody years between 1156 and 1160, when the Fujiwara were already in retreat, the Heike gained a brief ascendancy over the Minamoto and established their own emperors in court, but within a few years, they were overthrown by Yoritomo Minamoto in a series of epic battles that culminated in 1185 in the great sea coast battle at Dannoura. Within four years Yoritomo had eliminated the last resistance of the Fujiwara in the eastern provinces.

As shogun, or administrator general, Yoritomo established his own headquarters at Kamakura, three hundred miles east of Kyoto. A feeble court persisted in that city, but the Heian period was at an end. For the next seven hundred years Japan would be governed by military shoguns, mostly of Minamoto origin, who paid mere ceremonial homage to the emperors. (3)

At the beginning of the Kamakura era, three schools of Buddhism imported from China flourished in Japan—the Tendai, the Shingon, and the Pure Land. Dosho's Hosso sect had lost influence on the islands.

The Tendai School is considered the first wholly Chinese School of Buddhism. It had evolved as the result of confusion that had arisen in China long before Bodhidharma's voyage from the west. Often, Chinese travelers had brought back Buddhist documents from India, even though they could not read them, because it was believed the scrolls were inherently sacred. Often these documents were stored for many years before scholars arose who were able to translate them. The translators then discovered that some of the documents were only fragments and others had missing passages. More problematic was the fact that the documents reflected a wide range of perspectives within the long history of Indian Buddhism. The teachings proclaimed in one document might be difficult to reconcile with those in others, although they all purported to reflect the instructions of the Buddha. The founders of the

Tendai School set themselves the task of trying to determine which of these apparently contradictory teachings were those of the historic Buddha. They finally based their exposition of Buddhist doctrine on the *Lotus Sutra*, which they believed to be the least corrupt of the documents they had.

Although meditation was practiced in the Tendai tradition, the majority of Tendai adherents were satisfied with understanding it as a doctrinal system which was intellectually coherent and which was able to meet the devotional needs of the literate population.

Whereas the focus of the Tendai School was on scripture, the focus of the Shingon School was on ritual. It was one of the so-called "esoteric" schools of Buddhism, in which secret teachings, or "empowerments," were transmitted from teacher to student. These were not recorded in writing but were only available to initiates through oral instruction. The tradition was brought back to Japan by a monk named Kukai (better known by his posthumous name, Kobo Daishi) who accompanied one of the delegations from Japan to China in 804. Shingon practices included elaborate rituals and mantra recitation. A mantra is a special verbal formulation that the devotee keeps in mind. As a result of his practice with mantra, Kobo Daishi, it was claimed, acquired extraordinary powers of recall that allowed him to memorize all of the secret oral teachings that had been passed onto him in China.

The teachings that Kobo Daishi brought back to Japan survived there even after being eradicated in China during a persecution of Buddhism in that country in the mid-19th Century. Kobo Daishi did not intend to start a separate school of Buddhism but rather sought to enrich Buddhist practice. It would be his successors who would establish the school as an independent line of teaching. As the sect developed, the role of ritual became more central to it. Emperor Junna decreed that official rites for the state should be carried out in the Shingon Temple in Kyoto, and many influential families were drawn to the sect, hopeful that its rites would benefit them in their quest for political prominence.

The Pure Land Sect became popular among ordinary people who found philosophical Buddhism abstruse. Nor did traditional Shinto, which lacked a conception of personal immortality, have much to offer them; the blessings sought in Shinto ceremonies were not so much for personal attainment as for the benefit of the family and the clan. Buddhism, with its doctrine of reincarnation, offered hope to ordinary persons who found their lives burdensome. Daily difficulties, fear of brigandage, conflicts between warring clans, disease, and endless labor, gave the lower classes little to hope for in this life, prompting an understandable desire for a better life to come. The array of Buddhas and Bodhisattvas (roughly the equivalent of Buddhist saints) that had developed in devotional Buddhism provided a pantheon to whom individuals could offer prayers for personal health, achievement, or consolation in times of trial. The simplicity of the Pure Land School had great appeal; it taught that the repetition of a mantra dedicated to the Buddha Amida was adequate to ensure the devotee rebirth in the Pure Land, an albeit temporary heaven-like afterlife. The teaching had been brought to Japan in the 12th century CE by a monk named Honen, whose early training had been in the Tendai School.

In the Buddhism that had evolved in the centuries following the death of Siddhartha Gautama, it was recognized that there were many other "Buddhas" both in the past and yet to be born. Amida Buddha was the Buddha who reigned in the "Western Paradise." He had taken a vow that anyone who called upon him with faith would be reborn in that Paradise. Devotees were taught to repeat the *nembutsu*—"*Namu amida butsu*"—a short prayer meaning, "I take refuge in Amida Buddha." Later Zen teachers would occasionally advocate the practice of *nembutsu*, especially for the laity.

It was Honen's disciple, Shinran, who was primarily responsible for the spread of the Pure Land Buddhism. He began his religious career at Shorenji, the Tendai temple on Mount Hiei in Kyoto. His conversion to the Pure Land School came about as a result of a dream he had in which the Bodhisattva of Compassion appeared to him in the form of Prince Shotoku; the Bodhisattva told Shinran to seek out Honen and to dedicate himself to the practice of the *nembutsu*.

The rivalry between various schools of Buddhism was intense, and, in 1207, Shingon and Tendai leaders were able to have the Pure Land School officially proscribed. Honen and Shinran were both expelled from Kyoto. Now no longer a monk, although he did not consider himself a layman either, Shinran married and started a family.

The ban on the Pure Land School was lifted in 1211. Honen died a year later, so it was left to Shinran to revive the teaching. He decided not to return to Kyoto but instead worked from a small community just north of Edo. He proved to be an effective proselytizer, and through his efforts the teaching became popular among peasants and commoners. Today the Pure Land School is the most popular form of Buddhism in Japan.

MYOAN EISAI

Myoan Eisai was born in 1141. His father was a Shinto priest who had such respect for the new Buddhist religion that when his son was eight years old, he sent him to study at a Tendai temple on Mount Hiei overlooking Kyoto. Eisai took to his lessons well, and, at the age of fourteen, he was ordained in a ceremony during which his head was shaved and he "accepted the precepts"—the list of rules Buddhist monks agreed to abide by. Shaving the head was an act symbolic of renouncing all attachments as well as a public proclamation that the individual had committed himself to pursuing the Dharma.

After completing his training on Mount Hiei, Eisai undertook his first voyage to China in 1168, three years before Kakua, in order to further his studies. The visit was less than a year long, and, although during the course of it he met a number of Zen monks, he made no effort to question them about their teachings. He returned to Kyoto the following autumn, bringing with him a collection of Tendai texts written in Chinese. He dedicated the next twenty years of his life to the study of those texts, and found his interest piqued by the stories he read in them of various Zen teachers. He remained firmly committed to the Tendai tradition, however, and eventually earned the title of "Patriarch" within it.

In 1186, he made a second trip to China with the intention of undertaking a pilgrimage to important Buddhist sites in India. He had come to suspect that the Dharma taught in Japan may have been corrupted through mistranslations and contamination from non-Buddhist sources. He hoped that by traveling to the land of the Buddha's birth, he would find a purer expression of the Buddha's original teachings. However, once in China he was unable to procure the necessary travel documents to proceed to the sub-continent. Disappointed in his original intention, he decided to investigate the Zen school to see if it were a less adulterated expression of the Dharma than what was currently being promulgated in Japan. On Mount Tientai, he sought out Zen Master Kian Esho [Xuan Huai-chang] who belonged to the Rinzai [Ch: Linji] "House" of Zen.

Zen was not a homogeneous tradition in China. There were Five Houses each of which traced its lineage back to a particular group of teachers. The Rinzai House also produced two offshoots, which resulted in a total of Seven Schools. When Eisai visited China, the two strongest schools were the Rinzai and the Soto [Ch: Caodong].

While the goal of both of these is to guide practitioners to awakening, their approaches differ both in custom and focus. These differences reflect the personalities of the Tang dynasty teachers from whom they have descended. A basic difference in custom is that while meditators in the Soto tradition sit facing a wall (following the example of Bodhidharma), those in the Rinzai tradition sit facing into the room. A difference in focus can be found in the preferred mode of meditation. The Soto student is usually taught a subjectless meditation, known in Japanese as *shikan taza* or "just sitting."

For the Rinzai, students working with a teacher are generally given a series of koans upon which to meditate. The term koan [Ch: *gongan*] refers to a "public record," or "case," in the sense of the records kept by a court of law that establishes precedent in jurisprudence. Koans are generally based on stories of the teaching methods of the Zen Masters of the Tang Dynasty. In many instances the koan consists of a question posed by a student and the master's often apparently illogical reply. For example, when Joshu was once asked what the significance of Zen was, he replied, "The cypress tree in the garden." When Ummon was asked who the Buddha was, he said, "A dried shit-stick." (Sticks were used for personal hygiene.) The Rinzai student assigned such a koan meditated on it to discover for himself why the teacher's answer was appropriate.

The koan most students begin with is called Joshu's Dog. A student asked the 9th century Chinese master, "Does a dog have Buddha-nature?" Joshu replied, "*Mu!*" *Mu* literally means "no" or "nothing," and Joshu appears to contradict the generally accepted Buddhist belief that all things—not only dogs but even trees and stones—have "Buddha-nature." The meditator, however, is warned not to think of *mu* as meaning anything, but to absorb him or herself in the koan until he/she achieves the insight (*kensho*) that will allow them to successfully answer the teacher's question when he asks, "What is *mu*?"

The teaching techniques were not exclusive, so the Soto School made occasional use of koans, and Rinzai students could be advised to practice *shikan taza*. The Rinzai tradition had the reputation of being more demanding than the Soto and put a greater emphasis on attaining awakening. Soto practice was considered gentler and stressed the practice of sitting meditation (zazen) over attainment. What the schools shared was the belief that Buddhahood—awakening—is achieved not through study, acquiring knowledge of the teachings, but through direct spiritual experience.

What Eisai found in Rinzai Zen was something very different from the Buddhism with which he was familiar. It did not offer philosophical analysis or carry out ritual observances; rather, it focused on a discipline which, he was told, could bring him to have the same experience of awakening that Siddhartha Gautama had had 1600 years earlier. The goal of Zen was not to study Buddhism but to become a Buddha.

Eisai did koan study with Kian Esho for four years, following him from one monastery to another. In 1191, Eisai received official "transmission," acknowledgment that he had seen into his own Buddha-nature and was authorized to teach others. In recognition of this authorization, Kian Esho gave Eisai an official document that attested that Eisai was a successor in a tradition which was traced, without break, from the Buddha to the present day. He also presented his disciple with a robe, bowl, and a *hossu*—a short staff tufted with horse hair which represented the possessor's right to teach the Dharma, and, specifically in Eisai's instance, the authority to take and promote the Zen tradition to the people of Japan.

Although there had been Japanese who had studied Zen before him, Eisai is identified as the individual to establish Zen, in its Rinzai form, on the islands, just as Bodhidharma was acknowledged to have brought the meditation school to China. As with Bodhidharma, Eisai is also credited with introducing tea to a new land. Legend has it that Bodhidharma had been so angered after falling asleep during meditation one day that he cut off his eyelids, which fell to the earth and there, supposedly, grew to become the first tea plants. Eisai's story is less dramatic; he simply brought tea seeds back from China. Tea had been imported from China in small quantities before, but Eisai was the first to systematically cultivate tea plants in Japan. He even wrote a book in which he promoted tea as a helpful stimulant to meditation and good health. The beverage, at first, was better accepted than the new spiritual tradition he also brought from China.

His first attempt to establish a Zen temple was in Kyoto, where he ran into resistance from the clergy connected with other Buddhist sects active in the city. The Tendai hierarchy, perhaps considering Eisai an apostate, went to the court to prevent the introduction of what they called a "new sect" to the city. Eisai argued then, as he would throughout his life, that Zen was nothing "new," that, in fact, Saicho, the founder of the Tendai tradition, had practiced and taught meditation (zen). His adversaries were unswayed and remained opposed to his efforts.

Eisai found a sponsor, however, in Shogun Yoritomo and with his protection was able to found the first Zen temple in Japan, Shofukuji, at Hakata. Even in this remote region he had to defend the practice of Zen from the attacks of other schools. The basis of their objection was found in the traditional description of Zen attributed to Bodhidharma: Zen presented itself as a teaching "outside" the traditional scriptures, and Eisai described Zen as the "school of the Buddha mind." His opponents interpreted this as a specious claim to be a superior teaching without scriptural basis.

From Shofukuji, Eisai moved to the new capital at Kamakura. Yoritomo's son, the Shogun Yoriie, shared his father's admiration for Zen. They both found the spare and practical discipline of Eisai's teaching more appealing than the abstraction of other schools, and Yoriie continued his father's patronage of the new sect. At the request of both the Emperor and the Shogun, Eisai established a Zen temple, Kenninji, in Kyoto. The Shingon and Tendai schools of Buddhism resented the intrusion of the new meditation school in what was still the spiritual, if not currently the political, capital of Japan, and they retained enough influence to ensure that the new temple was obliged to serve their schools as well as the Zen tradition.

In spite of what others may have believed about him, Eisai had not rejected the Tendai tradition, and he continued to function within it as a priest. He maintained that Zen was a vehicle for renewing and strengthening Tendai Buddhism, which, to his mind, had become overly ritualistic. But he was also aware that he was a Dharma heir in the Rinzai lineage—the 53rd in a lineage he traced back beyond Bodhidharma to the Buddha himself. As a Rinzai master, he put an emphasis on awakening (kensho) which was not part of the Tendai tradition. For a time, at least, he would assert that Rinzai Zen was the fullest flowering of the Dharma.

In contrast to the luxury of other Buddhists temples in Japan, Eisai's temples were relatively poor. At one point, his monks had had nothing to eat for several days. Then a Buddhist devotee came to the temple and asked Eisai to have the monks chant sutras on his behalf (a common devotional practice). In payment for this service, he presented Eisai with two rolls of silk. The monks were elated, confident that the silk would be sold and the money used to resupply their larder. However, when a beggar came to Eisai seeking alms, Eisai gave him the rolls of silk. The monks were disappointed but, seeing that the master was eating no better than they were, kept their anger in check.

Then a second beggar came to the monastery. Because there was nothing else to offer, Eisai had the gold leaf stripped from the Buddha image and presented to the man. This time the monks, already irritable from hunger, protested what they considered amounted to a sacrilege. Eisai countered by telling them, "You're familiar with the stories told of the Buddha's prior lives before being born as Gautama Siddhartha. And you remember how time and again he gave up his life in order to help others. If he was so willing to do that, how can you imagine that he would object to giving up his halo for this man?"

After 1200, Eisai divided his time between the temples he had established in Kamakura and Kyoto. But he appears gradually to have returned to the Tendai tradition, remarking that it was not yet time for Zen to flourish in Japan. In his later years, he dedicated himself to Tendai ritualism. He died in 1215 at the age of 75.

Eisai was a synchronist. Whether it was by conviction or as a result of the times in which he lived, he presented Zen as supplemental to the more ceremonial and ritualistic forms of Buddhism popular among the upper classes of Japanese society. It was left to his disciples to begin the process of establishing Zen as a separate and autonomous school.

RYONEN MYOZEN

The most important of Eisai's Dharma heirs was Ryonen Myozen. When orphaned at the age of eight, he was placed in a Tendai temple on Mount Hiei where he studied under a monk named Myoyu. When Myozen was sixteen, he took the precepts in the Tendai tradition. He then sought to deepen his understanding of Buddhism by training with Eisai. Eventually he was recognized as Eisai's successor, and, after that teacher's death, Myozen continued to promote the Rinzai tradition and began to acquire his own disciples.

In 1223, Myozen planned to travel to China with several of his students. Before they left however, Myozen received word that his

Tendai teacher, Myoyu, was dying and had requested his former student come to see him one last time. Uncertain of where his obligation lay, Myozen called his monks together and put the situation to them. Should he proceed to China to deepen his Zen practice, or should he honor the debt he owed his teacher and go to his bedside? The majority of Myozen's students felt that the master's obligation to his teacher took priority and urged him to delay his trip to China and go to Myoyu. Only one student dissented, but his argument convinced Myozen to proceed with the trip. Myozen explained that the most effective way to discharge his debt to Myoyu would be to achieve awakening for the benefit of others. He stated that if he acquired:

> —even a trace of enlightenment, it will serve to awaken many people, even though it means opposing the deluded wishes of one person. If the virtue gained were exceptional, it would serve to repay the kindness of my teacher. (4)

Accompanied by the young monk who had encouraged him, Myozen set off for China. Once there the two parted company. Myozen proceeded to Mount Tientung, where Eisai had trained, and there he studied with two Chinese masters for three years. His health was not strong, however, and in May 1225, he died while seated in meditation.

The disciple who had encouraged Myozen to make the journey to China had pursued his own path while in the country, but before he returned to Japan he collected Myozen's ashes and brought them back with him. That's disciple's name was Dogen Kigen, and the other thing he brought to Japan from his visit to China was the Soto Zen tradition.

Portrait of Dogen

CHAPTER TWO

DOGEN KIGEN

Dogen Kigen was born in the year 1200. His ancestry was noble. His mother, Lady Motofusa, was a descendant of the powerful Fujiwara clan and was the concubine of Lord Minamoto Michichika, who served in the imperial household. Their son spent his earliest years in the rarefied atmosphere of the court. He was recognized as a precocious child who was able to read Chinese characters by the age of four. He had access to the best tutors available, and these provided the training considered suitable to one of his social standing.

Both of his parents died while Dogen was still a child. His father died when Dogen was two years old, and his mother became ill a few years later. She was a devout woman, and, during her final illness, she encouraged her son to spend his life wisely, to become a monk and seek a way to relieve the sufferings of humankind. Dogen was only eight years old when she died. As he sat beside her corpse during the official mourning period, he watched the smoke from a burning stick of incense rise into the air and dissipate. Observing it, he thought about his mother's words and was struck by the impermanence of all things.

An uncle adopted Dogen and took charge of his education. It was the uncle's intention that the boy would be his heir and serve in the imperial court. But at the age of thirteen, young Dogen ran away from the court to a member of his mother's family who was a student of Buddhism and magic. With the aid of this relative, Dogen was received as a novice at Enryakuji, the Tendai Monastery on Mount Hiei. It was during his ordination ceremony that he was given the Buddhist name Dogen, which means "Foundation of the Way." The young novice hoped that as a monk he would find answers to the questions he had been dwelling upon since his mother's funeral.

The normal training for Tendai novices focused on the study of Buddhist sutras. Dogen was well versed in the Chinese language and took to the study easily. But although he found wisdom in those scriptures, he still felt they were abstract and far removed from the actual world in which people were born, lived, suffered, and died.

The sutras asserted that all sentient beings had Buddha-nature, but this was accepted as a tenet of faith and was not understood as something one had to aspire to realize for oneself. For Dogen, however, that teaching posed a problem. If all beings had Buddha-nature and thus—as the Buddha himself declared at the time of his enlightenment—all beings were inherently perfect, then why had it been necessary for the Buddha to strive to attain awakening, and why had the old Indian, Bodhidharma, spent nine years gazing at a wall at Shaolin Monastery in China? If one were already a Buddha, why did the masters of old have to make such efforts to become aware of their Buddha-nature?

This problem obsessed Dogen; his biographers have described it as a natural koan that preoccupied him day and night. He presented his concern to a former Tendai monk, Koin. Koin had also come to the decision that enlightenment could not be attained through academic study and had dedicated himself to the path of Pure Land Buddhism, spending his time in the devout repetition of the *nembutsu*. Koin was unable to answer the younger man's questions, but he advised him to seek the counsel of Myoan Eisai, who had recently returned from China with teachings from the Zen school.

Dogen traveled to Kenninji and sought an audience with Eisai. He posed his question to the master, "If, as the scriptures assert, all of us already have the Buddha-nature, why is it that the masters of old had to struggle to attain awareness of it?"

Eisai told him, "No Buddha is conscious of having Buddha-nature, only the shallow are aware of it."

Dogen sensed something profound in that answer, and he asked to be admitted to the monastery. Eisai accepted him as a student. Within a year, however, Eisai died, and Dogen continued studying under Eisai's successor, Ryonen Myozen.

The Buddhism being taught in Kenninji was an amalgam of Tendai and Shingon with a little Chinese Zen mixed in. Dogen, who was drawn neither to the scholasticism of Tendai nor the ritualism of Shingon, hoped to have his doubts resolved through Zen teachings and practice. Although he had not yet come to Realization, his fervor was such that Myozen acknowledged him as one of his Dharma Heirs. When Myozen determined to follow the example of his master, Eisai, and travel to the Land of Song (as China was then called) in order to study with the Zen masters there, Dogen accompanied him.

They left for the Asian mainland in 1223. It was a rough crossing, and in his journal Dogen chronicled his seasickness and bouts of diarrhea. Once they landed at the port of Mingzhou, only Myozen was allowed to proceed. Dogen was confined to the ship and the dock for three months, perhaps because his papers were not in order or perhaps in medical quarantine. Although he was unable to move about, there was enough traffic at the docks that he learned a great deal about what was happening in the city and country. He was disappointed by what he learned of the apparent state of Buddhism in China. If Japanese Buddhism was still immature and caught up in ritualism and magical rites, the Buddhism of the Land of Song had grown stale and decrepit. Dogen worried that he might not find what he was looking for here.

Then in April, while still living on board the ship, Dogen met a cook (*tenzo*) from one of the Zen monasteries. The cook had come there hoping to purchase dried Japanese shiitake mushrooms from the ship's galley. Dogen was struck by the tenzo's deportment and wanted to quiz the monk about Zen practice. He invited the monk to remain on board that night as his guest. The tenzo declined, explaining that he was the head cook of his monastery and had to return to his duties.

"But would not spending your days in meditation be more profitable than cooking?" Dogen asked.

The tenzo gently suggested that the young Japanese visitor still did not know very much about Zen, and took his leave. Dogen was impressed by the tenzo's manner and felt more confident that there might yet remain a few pockets of pure Buddhism in China.

Once Dogen was allowed to leave the docks, he followed Myozen to the monastery at Tientong. There he was received by Master Musai Ryoha (Wuji Liaopai) of the Soto School, who introduced him to the practice referred to as "silent illumination" or *shikan taza*.

Dogen remained at Tientong after Myozen died in 1225. He admired the strict discipline that the monks adhered to, but he was angered that according to their regulations he—as a foreigner—was considered subordinate to native-born novices much younger than he. It was a particularly galling situation for one who had been raised as an aristocrat. He protested that he was Myozen's heir and that his rank should not be dependent upon his nationality. His protests were not well received and may have made his position at the monastery more difficult than it needed to have been.

When his situation failed to improve, Dogen left Tientong and embarked on a tour of other monasteries, still seeking the awakening or enlightenment experience that he only knew of from his reading. He also familiarized himself with the lineage charts of the various monasteries he visited and became well versed in the history of Chinese Zen. He would bring this respect for accurate records of transmission and succession back to Japan.

In the course of his travels, he had a second encounter with a tenzo. He found an elderly monk working in the heat of the day preparing food. The tenzo was hatless in the sun and walked barefoot over tiles which must have burned, but he showed no sign of discomfort. Dogen asked the monk how old he was, and the monk replied that he was approaching his seventieth year.

"Are there no younger monks who could assist you?" Dogen asked.

"Others are not me," the tenzo answered. "These are my duties, how can someone else fulfill them?"

"But surely there's no need to carry them out during the hottest period of the day," Dogen persisted.

"If not now, when?" the monk asked.

"I can see that you are a man of the way (Dao)," Dogen said. "Please tell me, what is the true Way?"

"The universe has never concealed it," the cook said and turned back to his work.

The conversation struck Dogen profoundly, and the memory of it would stay with him long after he returned to Japan.

Dogen came back to Tientong despite his displeasure over his status at the monastery. A new abbot had been installed, Tendo Nyojo (Tientong Rujing), and Dogen was greatly impressed by him. Here, he felt, was the "authentic" teacher for whom he had been searching. In later years, he would refer to Nyojo as the "Old Buddha." Nyojo was a voluble critic of the koan study current in the Chinese Rinzai School that had replaced all other forms of meditation and practice. Dogen would come to share this point of view. Nyojo stressed that formless seated meditation—*shikan taza*—was the preeminent Buddhist activity. For three years, Dogen stayed with him, dedicating himself to zazen and *shikan taza*.

Nyojo's sitting schedule was strenuous. Monks sat from early in the morning until late at night. When they showed signs of resistance, Nyojo upbraided them for the shallowness of their efforts, reminding them of the difficulties of the lives of those who lived outside the monastery, the long hours of labor demanded of farmers and other workers, the dangers associated with the life of a soldier.

The regular sitting schedule was even more onerous during the retreat periods known in Japanese as *sesshin*. During one such summer retreat, the monks were sitting late into the night, when Nyojo noticed that one had fallen asleep. He roused the monk, then admonished the group: "You must practice with all of your energy, even at the risk of your own lives. You must discard both body and mind!"

These words finally brought Dogen to a deep awakening. When it was time for the monks to attend *dokusan*, individual meetings with the teacher, Dogen strode into the room confidently and lit a stick of incense, an act reserved for rituals or significant celebrations.

"What is the point of this incense?" Nyogo demanded.

"I have discarded body and mind," Dogen said.

"You have discarded body and mind. Body and mind have indeed been discarded."

"Don't confirm me so easily," Dogen protested. "It may be no more than a temporary delusion."

"I'm not confirming you so easily," Nyojo said.

"Then show me you aren't."

"This is body and mind discarded," Nyojo said, demonstrating what he meant.

Dogen bowed.

"And that is discarding discarded," Nyojo remarked.

"The great matter of my life has been resolved," Dogen declared.

"It is no small thing for a barbarian (a foreigner) to come to such a great awakening," Nyojo told him.

Nyojo was so impressed with the depth of Dogen's awakening that he acknowledged the younger man as his Dharma Heir. Dogen stayed at the monastery for a while longer, deepening his understanding, and providing a model for future Japanese Soto and Rinzai masters who would remain in training long after their initial awakening.

Nyojo invited him to remain at Tientong as his assistant. Dogen was honored by the offer but declined it.

In 1227, he decided it was time to return to Japan and did so—as he put it—"with empty hands." Whereas previous visitors, like the monk Saicho, had returned from the Land of Song with copies of sutras and Buddhist artifacts, Dogen brought back only a portrait of Nyojo, the documents of succession which traced his teaching lineage back to Bodhidharma and beyond to the Buddha himself, and the ashes of Ryonen Myozen.

When asked what he had learned during his time in China, his self-deprecating reply was:

> —that the eyes are horizontal and the nose is vertical; thus I am unable to be deceived by others. There is not even a hair of Buddhism in me. Now I pass the time naturally. The sun rises in the east every morning, and every night the moon sets in the west. When the clouds clear, the outline of the mountains appears, and as the rain passes away, the surrounding mountains bend down. What is it after all? (5)

When he returned to Kenninji in Kyoto in order to bury Myozen's ashes, he was discouraged by what he found there. Living conditions, for example, were much more luxurious than the Spartan accommodations he had been familiar with in China. However, he did start to introduce others to the Zen teachings he had acquired, and it was here that he wrote a short work called *Fukanzazengi* (Universal Recommendations for the Practice of Zazen).

The *Fukanzazengi* is a primer on Zen practice. Dogen felt he was introducing Japanese students to true zazen practice for the first time, so the instructions he provided were very exact. One must, he wrote, follow the examples of the Buddha and Bodhidharma who both committed themselves to prolonged meditation practice.

> —you must suspend your attempts to understand by means of scrutinizing words, reverse the activity of the mind that seeks externally, and illuminate your own true nature. Mind and body will fall off spontaneously, and your original face will be revealed. . . .
>
> For zazen, you will need a quiet room. Eat and drink in moderation. Forget about the concerns of the day and leave such matters alone. Do not judge things as good or evil, and cease such distinctions as "is" and "is not." Halt the flow of the mind, and cease conceptualizing, thinking, and observing. Don't sit in order to become a Buddha, because becoming a Buddha has nothing to do with such things as sitting or lying down. (6)

He describes in detail the instructions for placing a cushion on a mat and sitting upon it in either the traditional full lotus posture (with legs crossed and both feet resting on the thighs of the opposite legs) or half-lotus posture (with only one foot resting on the opposite thigh). He describes the proper alignment of the body, how to hold the hands in the lap (thumb tips touching), and stresses the importance of keeping the eyes open. Finally one is to regulate the breath (taking long deep breaths, following a natural rhythm), and, sitting "firmly and resolutely," one thinks "about the unthinkable. How do you think about the unthinkable? Nonthinking. These are the essentials of zazen." (7)

As Dogen began to attract students, he also attracted the enmity of other schools of Buddhism; the Tendai even attempted to have their rivals suppressed by government intervention. Dogen chose to avoid confrontation and left Kyoto for a small community south of the city. There he found an abandoned hermitage, Anyoin, where he was free to gather disciples. As their number increased, a larger temple—dedicated to Kannon, the Bodhisattva of Compassion—was built to accommodate them. Soon Dogen was overseeing a growing monastic community. His chief disciple and head monk was Koun Ejo.

Later, at the invitation of a supporter, he relocated a third time to Fukui Prefecture north of Kyoto where he established Eiheiji. Although the original buildings have since been destroyed, Eiheiji remains, along with Sojiji, one of the two primary temples of the Soto Sect in Japan.

It was at Kannondori and Eiheiji that Dogen composed most of the essays that would later be brought together in his literary masterwork, the *Shobogenzo*. The title means "The True Eye of the Dharma"—the "eye of the Dharma" which, in the apocryphal tale, Gautama Buddha had passed on to the monk Kasyapa thus starting the Zen tradition.

The *Sobogenzo* is a collection of ninety-two essays on a wide variety of topics. It was written not in Chinese—the preferred ecclesiastical language of Buddhist writings in Japan —but in the vernacular. There are instructions on the proper form of meditation; there is a chapter of instructions to monastic cooks, doubtless inspired by the two tenzos Dogen had met in China; there are essays which express Dogen's understanding of basic Buddhist teachings.

Throughout the collection, Dogen maintains that practice and enlightenment are one. The Buddha had taught that all beings, just as they are, are whole and perfect, that all beings had "Buddha-nature" even though they were not aware of it. In a similar vein, Dogen asserts that while seated in meditation, enlightenment is present, even if the individual is unaware of it. All one needs to do is to forget the "self" (one's personality), and the larger Self (Buddha-nature) is present.

The essay entitled *Genjokoan*, provides an example of Dogen's style and teaching.

> Studying the Buddha Way is studying oneself. Studying oneself is forgetting oneself. Forgetting oneself is being enlightened by all things. Being enlightened by all things is causing the body-mind of oneself and the body-mind of others to be shed. There is ceasing the traces of enlightenment, which causes one to forever leave the traces of enlightenment which is cessation.
>
> When people first seek the Teaching, they are far from the bounds of the Teaching. Once the Teaching is properly conveyed in oneself, already one is the original human being. . . .
>
> People's attaining enlightenment is like the moon reflected in water. The moon does not get wet, the water isn't broken. Though it is a vast expansive light, it rests in a little bit of water—even the whole moon, the whole sky,

rests in a dewdrop on the grass, rests in even a single droplet of water. . . .

—when one rides a boat out onto the ocean where there are no mountains and looks around, it only appears round, and one can see no other, different characteristics. However, this ocean is not round, nor is it square—the remaining qualities of the ocean are inexhaustible. . . .

As a fish travels through water, there is no bound to the water no matter how far it goes; as a bird flies through the sky, there's no bound to the sky no matter how far it flies. While this is so, the fish and birds have never been apart from the water and the sky—it's just that when the need is large the use is large, and when the requirement is small the use is small. In this way, though the bounds are unfailingly reached everywhere and tread upon in every single place, the bird would instantly die if it left the sky and the fish would instantly die if it left the water. Obviously, water is life; obviously, the sky is life. There is bird being life. There is fish being life. There is life being bird, there is life being fish. There must be progress beyond this—there is cultivation and realization, the existence of the living one being like this. . . . In this way, if someone cultivates and realizes the Buddha Way, it is *attaining a principle, mastering the principle;* it is *encountering a practice, cultivating the practice.* (8)

As he became older, Dogen became more critical of the Rinzai School and its use of koans, and yet several of the essays in the *Shobogenzo* are based on classic koans. Dogen's criticism may have been based in part on his irritation over increased government support for the Rinzai School, or because Rinzai students could at times show more concern about passing koans than they were in understanding the teachings of Buddhism. On the other hand, he acknowledged his primary Dharma Heir, Koun Ejo, after Koun had resolved the koan "one thread [hair] passes through many holes."

For Dogen, zazen was *shikan taza*, just sitting rather than reflecting on koans. He had discovered in China that there were monks who had developed the ability to answer koans without actually attaining real insight; Dogen did not want this empty practice to emerge in Japan as well.

Dogen's health had never been robust, and while still in his early fifties he became seriously ill. He determined to go to Kyoto to seek medical treatment, and, suspecting he might not return, he first appointed Koun Ejo Abbot of Eiheiji in his place. Ejo then accompanied his master to Kyoto. On August 15, Dogen composed his death poem:

> Although I hope to see it once more in the autumn
> How can I sleep with such a moon this evening?

He died in Kyoto thirteen days later, at the age of 53.

Dogen, along with Hakuin Ekaku (born more than 400 years later), was one of the most significant figures in the history of Japanese Zen. The prominence of the Soto tradition both in Japan and North America is his legacy. But he was not always an easy man to deal with. He was subject to depression and could hold long resentments.

Whereas Eisai had sought to form alliances with influential figures in Kyoto and Kamakura, Dogen chose instead to stand aloof from such contacts. He preferred solitude and shunned the powerful. It was at least in part due to the prominence he acquired as a teacher that he left Kannon-dori and moved to the more isolated Eiheiji when the opportunity presented itself.

He was also a man who was aware of his own shortcomings. And when a group of students asked Dogen to tell them something about his life, he made this brief assessment: "Just one mistake after another."

"Circle, Triangle, Square" by Sengai Gibon

CHAPTER THREE

DOGEN'S SUCCESSORS

KOUN EJO

TETTSU GIKAI

GIEN

Koun Ejo, Dogen's close friend and heir, came to the Soto Zen tradition after first spending time in the "Daruma" school of Dainichi Nonin. This school claimed descent from the Chinese Rinzai tradition, although Myoan Eisai and others questioned its validity.

Dainichi Nonin was a contemporary of Eisai's who developed an interest in Buddhism at an early age. He was raised and trained in the Tendai Sect. He was a voracious reader and made a careful study of the various texts available to him. In particular, he was drawn to the descriptions he found of the meditation school brought to China by Bodhidharma (Daruma in Japanese). Following instructions he was able to glean from his reading, Nonin committed himself to the practice of meditation and achieved what he believed to be a genuine kensho. He set himself up as a teacher at Sanbo Temple (Sanboji), attached to the Tendai center in Settsu, and called his new school the "Daruma School" in honor of the first patriarch of Chinese Zen.

Although he was able to gather students who were interested in learning the practice of meditation, Nonin was conscious that he lacked official recognition of his enlightenment. So in the year 1189 he sent two of his disciples to visit the Rinzai master, Zhuoan Deguang, in China taking with them a letter in which Nonin asked the master to authorize his right to teach. Surprisingly, Zhuoan sent back a letter affirming the validity of Nonin's awakening and presenting him with a "Dharma robe," a traditional symbol of transmission.

Myoan Eisai did not receive transmission from Kian Esho until two years later, 1191, and when he returned to Japan, Eisai was dismissive of the Daruma School. Zen tradition in China insisted on mind-to-mind transmission between teacher and student, therefore the written authorization Nonin had received from Zhuoan was questionable.

Nonin was unfazed by his critics and continued to teach. Following the traditions he had read about, he even named a Dharma successor, Bucchi Kakuan. Kakuan left Sanboji to establish his own meditation center at Tonomine. In spite of the controversy over Nonin's status, and thus that of his heirs, the Daruma School acquired some fame, and a number of individuals important in the history of Japanese Buddhism became Kakuan's disciples. Among these were the monks Gien, Tettsu Gikai, and Koun Ejo.

KOUN EJO

Ejo was born into an aristocratic family and received a Buddhist education in the Tendai tradition as a matter of course. He may have been an over-sensitive child and was drawn to enter religious life at an early age, driven by a sense of his personal shortcomings. This sense of unworthiness was something with which Ejo would struggle throughout his entire life. Years later, while an Abbot and heir of Dogen, he would describe himself in a poem as:

> Weighted down with karma and a despicable character,
> By far the first among humans in sinfulness.
> Barefoot he learned to walk.
> Before he wore out his sandals, he saw his original self. (9)

In 1218, at the age of 20, he received the precepts from Master Enno of the Yokawa Tendai temple on Mount Hiei. He also studied the Shingon tradition. The monks on Mount Hiei lived comfortably and were held in high esteem. There was a hierarchy within which the monks sought to rise, accumulating social status as they did so. Ejo found himself gaining stature in this milieu and did not question it until his mother challenged him. She asked him pointedly: "Did you become a monk in order to be able to hobnob with the well-to-do? That's not why I supported your desire to enter the monastery. You should not pursue these studies for the wealth or status they can bring you. My desire is that you commit yourself sincerely, practicing in poverty, without worldly ambition."

Ejo realized he had strayed from his original intentions, and he left Mount Hiei, turning his back on both the Tendai and Shingon communities. He worked with a teacher in the Pure Land tradition for a while, practicing the *nembutsu*, then went to Tonomine and asked Kakuan to accept him as a student. Working with Kakuan, Ejo resolved some of his personal problems and achieved an initial awakening. Then sectarian rivals burned down Tonomine and its students scattered. Ejo was one of several who sought out Dogen at Kenninji.

Ejo had been well respected in the Daruma School and had come to an awakening under Kakuan's instruction. He had also had extensive training in the Tendai, Shingon, and Pure Land traditions. In addition, at thirty-one years old he was Dogen's senior by two years; so to some extent, he and Dogen met as equals. They immediately liked one another, and spent two days in discussions about the Dharma, finding themselves in agreement on every point raised. However, on the third day, Dogen, now confident of Ejo's sincerity, felt he could begin to speak more directly. He identified the areas where their perspectives differed. Ejo was discouraged that Dogen, who was obsessed with the legitimacy of lineage documentation, questioned the validity of his awakening experience and the practices of the Daruma School. In spite of this, it was clear to Ejo that Dogen respected him. Ejo remained certain that his awakening had been genuine; however, he also recognized that, compared with Dogen's, his understanding was shallow. He hoped that Dogen could help him deepen it.

In a rigidly hierarchal society like that of Medieval Japan, it would have been unusual for someone older to ask a younger man to accept him as a student, but Ejo was humble enough and admired Dogen sufficiently to do so. To Ejo's dismay, however, Dogen declined as politely as circumstances allowed, telling Ejo that conditions were not yet right at Kenninji for teaching the Dharma. He told Ejo that he would later seek a more appropriate and permanent temple where he would promote the practice of Zen in Japan, and he invited Ejo to visit him there once it was established.

After this first meeting with Dogen, Ejo went on a pilgrimage of Buddhist monasteries in Japan, and eventually returned to a settlement near the ruins of Tonomine, where Kakuan was still living. Ejo remained with Kakuan, caring for him, until the latter's death.

The Daruma School had not died out entirely. Some of Kakuan and Nonin's students continued to study with the new head of the school, a monk named Ekan. Ejo, too, may have studied with Ekan for a while. Among the other monks who studied with Ekan were Gikai and Gien.

Just before his death, Kakuan advised Ejo to approach Dogen once again and ask to be accepted as a disciple. By then Dogen had established his training center at Kannondori, and there, in 1234, Ejo was finally accepted as a disciple. Later, Ekan and several of his students also joined Dogen's community of monks.

At this point in his career, Dogen was still using koans as a teaching means, and he assigned Ejo the koan: "One thread [hair] pierces many holes." Ejo focused his attention on the koan for a long while. He remained baffled by it until, one day, as he was setting out his food bowls, he suddenly resolved it. He rushed to Dogen's rooms and bowed ceremoniously.

"Have you understood something?" Dogen asked.

"I don't ask about the one thread, but what of the many holes?" Ejo replied.

"Pierced!" Dogen said with a laugh.

Now satisfied with Ejo's level of understanding, Dogen appointed him head monk of the community. Ejo also served as Dogen's personal attendant, and, when Dogen established Eiheiji, Ejo was put in charge of the daily operations of the temple.

During his final illness, before he went to Kyoto to seek medical attention, Dogen first appointed Ejo his heir, pointing out that although Ejo was older than he, Ejo would outlive his teacher by many years. At the same time, Dogen put Tettsu Gikai in charge of operations. As Ejo had been before him, Gikai was now responsible for the running of the monastery and overseeing its religious and ritual responsibilities; Ejo, as Dogen's heir, would be in charge of the formation and teaching of the monks.

After Dogen's death, Ejo was formally installed as the second abbot of Eiheiji. He brought Dogen's ashes back to Eiheiji and had them interred in a memorial pagoda. It was Ejo's goal to preserve, as well as he could, Dogen's Zen as it was presented in the *Shobogenzo* and his personal teachings. Ejo collected his master's writings and perhaps spent too much time working on these. As a result, he may not have realized the extent to which discipline in the monastery had begun to suffer, nor may he have been aware that a division was growing among the monks that would become more serious as time passed. It is also possible that his continued sense of personal unworthiness kept him from growing into the type of leader the community needed.

TETTSU GIKAI

Ejo recognized Gikai as his own heir because he believed that Dogen would have wanted him to do so. However, although Ejo was aware of the respect Dogen had had for Gikai, Ejo himself had some reservations about him. He suspected that, like many of the former Daruma School members, Gikai held beliefs, in particular about the so-called esoteric or ritual practices, which were inconsistent with what Ejo understood to be Dogen's Zen. Ejo reminded Gikai that zazen was the singular focus of Dogen's teaching. Ejo knew there were members of the sangha at Eiheiji who did not believe that zazen was necessarily the only appropriate form of practice, so he questioned Gikai about where he stood on the issue. Gikai admitted that, while he valued the practice of zazen, he believed there were other disciplines that could be just as valuable to one's religious development. Ejo pressed the issue, and Gikai at least gave the impression that his opinion was swayed.

To deepen Gikai's understanding of Zen, Ejo encouraged him to go on a tour of other monasteries in Japan. Gikai went even further and, on his own initiative but with Ejo's permission, traveled to China as well. He was impressed by the depth of the established Zen tradition and its trappings in the Land of Song and was awed by both the architecture and the furnishings of the temples he visited. He made detailed copies of the architectural designs of these sites and collected cultic items to bring back to Japan.

When Gikai returned to Eiheiji, Ejo appointed him abbot and retired. Ejo settled in a hermitage not far from the temple, hoping to pass his final days in solitude; however, some of his former students, uncomfortable with Gikai, visited Ejo on a regular basis. It soon became clear that there was a division between a group of monks who supported Gikai and another group that wanted Ejo to return. Gikai, this latter group complained, was less interested in the spiritual development of the monks than he was in transforming Eiheiji architecturally and making it a place of elaborate shrines. He also had never wholly given up his belief that zazen was not necessarily the only appropriate practice, and ritual elements were gradually being introduced into the monks' daily schedule of activities. There were also questions raised about a subsidiary temple he had built for the care of his mother.

In 1272, the faction that opposed Gikai persuaded Ejo to return and resume the position of Abbot. Gikai withdrew his claim to the post rather than cause further divisions within the community, although he remained at Eiheiji and continued to work with Ejo.

Ejo tried to reconcile the divisions that had arisen at Eiheiji, but went to his death feeling that he had failed to do so and, thus, had failed in his responsibilities to his teacher, Dogen.

Just before he died, Ejo commanded his students not to build a memorial pagoda for him but simply to bury him at the foot of Dogen's pagoda.

After Ejo's death, Gikai was returned to the position of Abbot, but the divisions within the community remained unresolved. For the traditionalists, the final straw came when Gikai complied with a government request that Shingon rituals be carried out at Eiheiji for the benefit of the country.

The Government directive had come about because they sought divine aid in their efforts to resist the intentions of the Mongol leader, Kublai Khan, to add Japan to his vast conquests. The Khan had already taken control of both China and Korea. Eight years earlier he had sent a number of delegations to the Japanese isles demanding that they too acknowledge his leadership. After hearing what the first messengers had to say, the Japanese prevented later delegations from landing on the island of Honshu.

In 1274, when Ejo was serving his second term as abbot of Eiheiji, the offended Khan mobilized a fleet of more than 500 ships and an army of 40,000 soldiers to conquer the impudent Land of Wa. The Japanese defense force was considerably smaller, estimated at no more than 10,000 samurai.

When the Mongol forces landed in November, the samurai fought valiantly in what was clearly a hopeless cause. After the first day of battle, the samurai withdrew from the beachhead to rest and recover their strength. They fully intended to resume the fight in the morning, although it was almost certain they would be annihilated.

However, during the night, the Mongol forces reboarded their ships and sailed out into the bay because the sailors were afraid that the high winds that had arisen might drive their ships onto shore and ground them. That decision was a grave error; the Mongol fleet sailed directly into the path of a typhoon that sank a third of the boats, drowning their crews and passengers. The remaining vessels were heavily damaged and forced to retreat back to China.

The Japanese believed that the wind—which they termed "Kamikaze" or "divine wind"—was evidence that the old Shinto gods still protected the isles. Seven years later, during Gikai's second term as abbot of Eiheiji, the Japanese learned that Kublai Khan was preparing a second invasion of their homeland. This time the Khan had amassed a force five times larger than the previous one—two fleets of more than 4000 ships and an estimated 140,000 soldiers. In the face of this armada, government officials ordered all

Buddhist Temple to perform rites for the protection of the country. The rites probably had little to do with it, but once again the Khan's forces were destroyed by a typhoon. After this second defeat, he gave up his intentions to subjugate the archipelago.

In spite of the national emergency, the traditional forces at Eiheiji resisted the inclusion of Shingon rites at their temple. Gikai, on the other hand, believed that not only should they comply with the government request but that by adding these ritual elements the Soto School would be likely to become more popular with the Japanese laity. Those in disagreement with him, however, held that Master Dogen would never have approved of these changes. There were strong feelings on both sides of the issues, and violence broke out between Gikai's supporters and his opposers. Gikai fled the temple in remorse over the conflict he had caused and possibly in fear of his own safety.

GIEN

With Gikai out of the way, another former member of the Daruma School and student of Ekan, Gien, was appointed abbot. He was officially designated the third abbot of Eiheiji, after Dogen and Ejo. The seven-year period during which Gikai had served in that position was discounted.

Gikai sought refuge at the Shingon temple, Daijoji, where he was able to establish a community that combined both Shingon and Zen practices.

Gien, possibly because of his previous involvement with the Daruma School, was unable to resolve the factions within his community. And when, in 1297, a fire destroyed several buildings in the monastery complex, Gien did not have the financial resources to rebuild it. Many monks left Eiheiji to seek other monasteries, and Gien himself retired to a hermitage.

Within two generations of Dogen's death, both Eiheiji and the Soto School of Zen seemed in tatters. It would be later men who would rebuild both, and the form of Soto that would gain dominance would descend from a man recognized as the heir of both Gien and Gikai.

Zen-style landscape painting by Tani Buncho (1763-1840)

CHAPTER FOUR

CHINESE CONNECTIONS

BUKKO KOKUSHI

CHIYONO [MUGAI NYODAI]

ENNI BEN'EN [SHOICHI KOKUSHI]

MUKAN FUMON

SHINCHI KAKUSHIN

NAMPO JOMYO [DAIO KOKUSHI]

Bukko Kokushi

The Japanese Zen master, Bukko Kokushi, was born in China. His Buddhist name was Wuxue Zuyuan, which the Japanese pronounced Mugaku Sogen. The name Bukko was given to him posthumously, according to the common custom, along with the title Kokushi, which means "National Teacher."

Bukko became a monk at the age of 13 and studied with the Zen Master, Mujun Shiban (Wuzhun Shifan) (10). Shiban was one of the most significant Chinese teachers of his day, and one of the few who was willing to accept Japanese students. In addition to being a master of the Rinzai tradition, Shiban was also a celebrated artist and calligrapher, and his students acquired an appreciation of those along with their Zen training.

Shiban assigned Bukko the koan "Mu." Bukko, a self-confident young man, was certain he would be able to resolve the koan within a year. But after six years had passed, he still had not made any headway with it. Then, as he reported later, "while no special change came over me, the 'Mu' became so inseparably attached to me that I could not get away from it even while asleep. This whole universe seemed to be nothing but the 'Mu' itself." (11)

Shiban recognized the difficulty Bukko was having and advised him to leave Mu aside for a while and practice *shikan taza* instead. However, by then Bukko was so deeply absorbed in Mu that he was unable to withdraw his attention from it although he still had no idea what it signified. He reported that Mu was so powerful that at times he did not know whether he was sitting or standing. He persisted in the practice for another six months; then, on hearing a block of wood struck, he came to awakening.

He wrote this description of what happened:

Thence my joy knew no bounds. I could not quietly sit in the Meditation Hall; I went about with no special purpose in the mountains, walking this way and that. I thought of the sun and moon traversing in a day through a space 4,000,000,000 miles wide. "My present abode is China," I reflected then, "and they say the district of Yang is the center of the earth. If so, this place must be 2,000,000,000 miles away from where the sun rises; and how is it that as soon as it comes up its rays lose no time in striking my face?" I reflected again, "The rays of my own eye must travel just as instantaneously as those of the sun as it reaches the latter; my eyes, my mind, are they not the Dharmakaya itself?" Thinking thus, I felt all the bounds snapped and broken to pieces that had been tying me for so many ages. How many numberless years had I been sitting in the hole of ants! Today even in every pore of my skin there lie all the Buddha-lands in the ten quarters! I thought within myself, "Even if I have no greater satori [awakening], I am now all-sufficient unto myself." (12)

After his enlightenment, Bukko became head priest of his own temple. At that time, the Mongols were completing their conquest of China, and enemy soldiers scoured the countryside looking to suppress pockets of resistance. A group of these raided Bukko's temple, intending to put all the monks there to death as they had elsewhere. Bukko remained calm in the face of the attack and asked the leader of the soldiers to allow him time to compose a poem to mark the occasion of his death. While the soldiers waited with drawn swords, Bukko took up his calligraphy brush and wrote:

In all this world there is no place for me to lay down my staff
Subject and object are totally empty! How delightful!
The great sword of a famous warrior of the past—
It is as if a spring breeze were split by a bolt of lightning.

Impressed by the equanimity with which the monk faced his impending death, the soldiers retreated without harming any of the members of the community.

Word of the encounter between Bukko and the Mongol soldiers reached the current leader of Japan—Hojo Tokimune. Tokimune was the *shikken*, or regent, to the Shogun, but in fact held the reins of power in the country. His father, Tokiyori, had been a Zen practitioner and came to enlightenment under the guidance of a Chinese Zen master teaching in Japan. Tokimune was credited with repelling the first attempt made by the Monguls to invade Japan, but he realized it had only been good fortune that had prevented the invasion from succeeding. He fully expected the Monguls to make a second attempt, and, to help him prepare for that, Tokimune invited Bukko to come to Japan in 1279 to serve as his teacher.

Bukko, who was 56 years old at the time, accepted the invitation. He asked Tokimune what it was he was seeking from the practice of Zen. Tokimune explained that he sought to conquer all fear. Bukko instructed him to search within himself for the source of fear; this became Tokimune's koan—"Where is my fear located?"

When the second Mongol fleet approached Japan, Tokimune went to see Bukko and told him, "This will be the most important event in my life."

"And how do you plan to deal with it?" Bukko asked.

Tokimune responded by shouting out the word "Victory!" with all his might.

"Ah," Bukko remarked. "The son of a lion roars like a lion!"

After the failure of the second Mongul invasion, Tokimune built Engaku Temple as a memorial for all those who had lost their lives defending Japan. Bukko was installed as its first head priest.

Bukko was the teacher who brought the Zen tradition to the samurai. Seeing the esteem Tokimune had for him, samurai warriors were drawn to the Zen master as well. In spite of the Buddhist prohibition against taking life, Bukko did not condemn the samurai for being warriors; after Tokimune died, Bukko even declared that the *shikken* had been a Bodhisattva. The samurai saw Zen not so much as a religion but rather as a practical discipline with which they learned to overcome their fears and face death with equanimity.

CHIYONO [MUGAI NYODAI]

One of Bukko's students was the first Japanese woman to receive a certificate of *inka*. Her Buddhist name was Mugai Nyodai, but she is remembered by her personal name, Chiyono. She was a member of the Hojo family by marriage and a well-educated woman who long had an interest in the Dharma. After her husband died and her family responsibilities had been fulfilled, she went to study with the Chinese master. After completing her studies with Bukko, she became the founding abbess of the most important Zen temple for women in Kyoto, Keiaiji.

A teaching story with no apparent basis in fact suggests that before coming to study with Bukko, Chiyono had been a servant at a small temple where three nuns practiced Buddhism and hosted evening meditation sessions for the laity. According to this story, Chiyono observed the people practicing zazen and tried to imitate their sitting in her quarters, but without any formal instruction all she acquired for her efforts were sore knees. Finally she approached the youngest of the nuns and asked how to do zazen.

The nun replied that her duty was to carry out her responsibilities to the best of her abilities. "That," she said, "is your zazen."

Chiyono felt she was being told not to concern herself with things that were beyond her station. She continued to fulfill her daily tasks, which largely consisted of fetching firewood and hauling buckets of water. She noticed, however, that people of all classes joined the nuns during the meditation sessions; therefore, there was no reason why she, too, could not practice. This time she questioned the oldest of the nuns. This woman provided Chiyono with basic instruction, explained how to sit, place her hands, fix her eyes, and regulate her breathing.

"Then, drop body and mind," she told Chiyono. "Looking from within, inquire 'Where is mind?' Observing from without, ask 'Where is mind to be found?' Only this. As other thoughts arise, let them pass without following them and return to searching for mind."

Chiyono thanked the nun for her assistance, then lamented that her responsibilities were such that she had little time for formal meditation.

"All you do can be your zazen," the nun said, echoing what the younger nun had said earlier. "In whatever activity you find yourself, continue to inquire, 'What is mind? Where do thoughts come from?' When you hear someone speak, don't focus on the words but ask, instead, 'Who is hearing?' When you see something, don't focus on it, but ask yourself, 'What is that sees?'"

Chiyono committed herself to this practice day after day. Then, one evening, she was fetching water in an old pail. The bucket, held together with bamboo which had weakened over time, split as she was carrying it and the water spilled out. At that moment, Chiyono became aware.

Although the story about her time as a servant is certainly apocryphal, the part about the broken pail precipitating her enlightenment seems to be based on her actual experience. She commemorated the event with these lines:

In this way and that I tried to save the old pail
Since the bamboo strip was weakening and about to break
Until at last the bottom fell out.
No more water in the pail!
No more moon in the water! (13)

ENNI BEN'EN [SHOICHI KOKUSHI]

Although Zen teachers—immigrants as well as native born—
could now readily be found in Japan, some of the more serious
students still felt it necessary to travel to China to get the training they wanted. One of these was Enni Ben'en, also known by
the posthumous name, Shoichi Kokushi—Shoichi, the National
Teacher

The syncretic Zen of Myoan Eisai, a combination of the Chinese Rinzai tradition and Tendai, was short-lived in Japan. It would
be the form of Rinzai brought back to the islands from China by
Shoichi that would persevere.

During his lifetime Enni Ben'en was admired both for his extensive erudition and the depth of his enlightenment. Like Eisai
and Gikai, later in his life Enni was willing to make accommodations for other Buddhist traditions; however, as a young man he
was not so flexible.

His early training had been a mixture of Tendai and Confucianism. Then he went to Chorakuji to study with one of Myoan
Eisai's disciples, the monk Eicho. Like that of Eisai before him,
Eicho's Buddhism was a combination of Tendai and Zen. Enni
decided that he wanted to experience a Zen unadulterated by other
traditions, so went to China where he was accepted as a student
by Mujun Shiban. Enni studied under Shiban's direction for seven
years and came to enlightenment in 1237.

After his awakening, Enni returned to Japan, fully familiar with Chinese monastic discipline. For a time, he taught in a temple located in the port city of Hakata on Kyushu, the southernmost of the Japanese isles. There he encountered the same hostility Zen and Pure Land teachers were still receiving from other Buddhist sects in Kyoto; although Shingon and Tendai animosity did not prevent him from teaching, it did frustrate him because he held both traditions in esteem.

When the retired statesman, Kujo Michiie, determined to build a temple in Kyoto, he recruited Enni as its abbot. That temple, Tofukuji, is today designated one of Japan's national treasures. While in Kyoto, Enni also served as abbot of Eisai's Kenninji. He divided his time between the two temples, walking from one to the other every day.

Tofukuji, as envisioned by Michiie, was to be a place where the Zen, Shingon, and Tendai traditions could co-exist. Enni, who had had training in the other two schools as well, was able to preside over the rituals associated with all three, but he gave precedence to the Zen practice of meditation.

Zen, he told his disciples, was not a system of thought like the other traditions but was the vehicle by which one achieved the same state of mind as the Buddha himself. "When one practices Zen, one is Buddha! If one practices for a day, one is Buddha for a day. If one were to practice one's whole life, one would be Buddha one's whole life."

Zen is the Buddha mind. The precepts (morality) are its external form; the teachings [sutras] are its explanation in words; the invocation of the name (*nembutsu*) is an expedient means (*upaya*). Because these three proceed from the Buddha mind, this school [Zen] represents the foundation. (14)

The Chinese form of Rinzai that Enni promoted took an aggressive approach to zazen. Students were advised to put all their energy into their practice: "Imagine that you've fallen into a deep well. In such a situation, your only thought would be how to escape. All your attention, all your energy would be focused on that alone. Day and night, all you would dwell on was how to escape."

The use of koans gave an energy to meditation not always present in the Soto practice of *shikan taza*. In a popular formula, three components were deemed necessary to achieve awakening: Great Faith, Great Perseverance, and Great Doubt. Great Doubt was the driving question that compelled one's practice—such as Dogen's question about why one needed to sit zazen if one were already, as the Buddha had proclaimed, enlightened. Koans forced the practitioner to approach his or her meditation with an inquiring frame of mind, and that spirit of questioning proved to be an effective tool—a "skillful means" or *upaya*—for arousing the "Great Doubt" needed to bring aspirants to awakening.

In spite of the preferential status he gave Zen, Enni also honored the Shingon and Tendai teachings and was thus eventually able to win respect for the Zen school, which was beginning to be seen less as a Chinese oddity and more of a mainstream tradition in Japan. But Enni understood that Zen was still young in Japan, and he continued to encourage his disciples to travel to China to deepen their practice.

Enni's Rinzai was not yet a school independent of Shingon and Tendai teachings, but it was Zen on its way to independence from those traditions.

Enni's fame spread throughout the land, and word about him came to the Imperial Household. Michiie arranged for Enni to have an audience with the Emperor Go-Uda. [The prefix "Go" means "later" and was appended to the name of an Emperor whose posthumous name was the same as that given to a previous emperor.] During the interview, Enni presented the Emperor with a volume of teachings from the Chinese Zen masters. The emperor was so impressed by the book that he later took the precepts from Enni and became a Buddhist.

During his 79th summer, Enni ordered the temple drums to be sounded and announced to his disciples that he was going to die. He then wrote a farewell poem, in which he stated: "Those who do not see things as they are will never understand Zen." Then he bid his disciples farewell and passed away.

MUKAN FUMON [DAIMIN KOKUSHI]

Enni Ben'en's school continued to receive the support of the court after his death. His heir, Tozan, was appointed spiritual advisor to the Emperor Fushimi (1287-1298), and Emperor Hanazono (1308-1318) bestowed upon Enni the posthumous name and title Shoichi Kokushi.

A later descendent of Shoichi, Mukan Fumon, performed a service for the Emperor Go-Kameyama (1383-1392) for which he too would be awarded the title Kokushi. According to the story, the Emperor's palace had become haunted, and he called upon various priests to exorcise the ghosts without success. His advisors suggested he seek the assistance of Fumon. Called to the court, Fumon told the Emperor, "The honored Confucius, whose writings we consider secular and not religious, wrote that demons and ghosts are helpless before men of virtue. My monks and I can dispose of them without difficulty." Then Fumon and several of his disciples took up residence in the palace. Unlike the earlier priests who had tried to rid the palace of its unwanted occupants by magic rites and religious ceremonies, Fumon did not perform any particular rituals; he did not even chant the sutras, as was common for Buddhists. He and his monks simply sat quietly and persistently in zazen. The ghosts dispersed. The Emperor was so impressed that he declared the palace a Zen monastery and appointed Fumon its abbot.

Shinchi Kakushin

Shinchi Kakushin was a contemporary of Enni Ben'en. He attended a Buddhist school associated with the local Shinto shrine and became a monk at the age of 19. When he had his head shaved, he was given the Buddhist name "Kakushin" which means "Enlightened Mind."

In 1235, he became interested in Zen after meeting Gyoyu Zenji, one of Myoan Eisai's heirs. Four years later, he accompanied Gyoyu to Jufukuji in Kamakura, where Gyoyu put him in charge of the operations of the temple.

After Gyoyu's death. Kakushin studied for a while with Dogen, but ultimately decided that he needed to go to China to better understand Zen. There he had hoped to study with Mujun Shiban as had Bukko Kokushi and Shoichi, but Shiban had recently died.

Instead, Kakushin became a student of Mumon Ekai (Wumen Huikai—cf. *Zen Masters of China*, Chapter Twenty-One) the famed author of the koan collection entitled *The Mumonkan, or Gateless Gate*.

When Kakushin presented himself before Mumon, the master challenged him by saying, "There is no gate into my temple. Where did you enter?"

"I entered through no-gate (*wu-men*)," Kakushin retorted.

"And what is your name?"

"My name is Enlightened Mind [Kakushin]!"

Wumen was so pleased with this exchange that he composed a poem on the spot,

> Mind, just this is Buddha.
> Buddha, just this is Mind.
> Mind and Buddha, thus, thus,
> In the past and now. (15)

Under Mumon's direction, Kakushin was introduced to koan practice. He achieved awakening after only six months in China, and won the admiration of his teacher. When it was time for him to return to Japan, Mumon presented him with a hand-written copy of the *Mumonkan*. It was the first copy to come to Japan.

Back in his homeland, Kakushin served at various temples where he trained students using the koans in Mumon's collection. He also gave public lectures on the first koan in the series—Joshu's Mu. He was invited to speak on Buddhism to both the reigning and the retired emperors. When the Emperor Go-Uta asked about Zen, Kakushin told him: "A Buddha is one who understands mind. The ordinary fellow does not understand mind. You cannot achieve this by depending upon others. To attain Buddhahood you must look into your own mind."

Kakushin was likewise the teacher of the samurai, Yoritake Ryoen. Yoritake was said to have attained enlightenment after hearing the sound of a flute following a battle. Under Kakushin's direction he was able to use the music of the flute to bring others to awakening. The sect they founded in this way was known as Fuke. The practitioners of Fuke included samurai and other lay people who made use of a distinctive headgear that included a basket-like covering of the face. In later years, highwaymen and other criminals would wear this headgear as a way of disguising their features and consequently the sect would eventually be banned. Long before that, however, through the guidance of men like Kakushin and Bukko Kokushi, Zen became the religion of the samurai.

NAMPO JOMYO

Nampo Jomyo was another who traveled to China to deepen his understanding of Zen.

He was the nephew of Enni Ben'nen and became a monk at the age of 15. Three years later, at 18, he sought out the Chinese master Rankei Doryu [Lanxi Daolong] who had come to Japan to establish Kenchoji as a Rinzai temple in Kamakura. After a time with Rankei, Jomyo went to China to continue studying with Kido Chigu [Xutang Zhiyu], Rankei's Dharma brother.

In 1265, Jomyo achieved enlightenment and was recognized as an heir by Kido. Kido was so impressed by the young Japanese's attainment that when the time came for him to return to his home country, Kido wrote this valedictory poem predicting the success he would find in Japan:

> To knock on the door and search with care,
> To walk broad streets and search the more:
> Old [Kido] taught so clear and bright,
> And many are the grandchildren on the
>   eastern sea who received [this teaching]. (16)

Upon his return to Japan, Jomyo spent some time with his former teacher, Rankei, before moving to the southern island of Kyushu, where he was appointed abbot of Kotokuji and later of Sofukuji, where he taught for thirty years.

In 1304 he was invited to Kyoto by the retired Emperor, Go-Uda in order to become the abbot of Kagenji; however, the continued enmity of the Tendai hierarchy to the incursions of Zen temples into their city prevented him from staying.

His final temple was Kenchoji in Kamakura. At his investiture ceremony, he is said to have proclaimed, "My coming today is coming from no where. One year hence, my departing will be departing to no where."

Just as he predicted, one year to the day he died. The death poem he left behind reads:

> I rebuke the wind and revile the rain,
> I do not know the Buddha and patriarchs;
> My single activity turns in the twinkling of an eye,
> Swifter even than a lightning flash. (17)

Like Bukko, Jomyo was given a posthumous name, Daio, and the title, National Teacher. The most vigorous line of the Japanese Rinzai School would proceed from the Dharma descendents of Daio Kokushi.

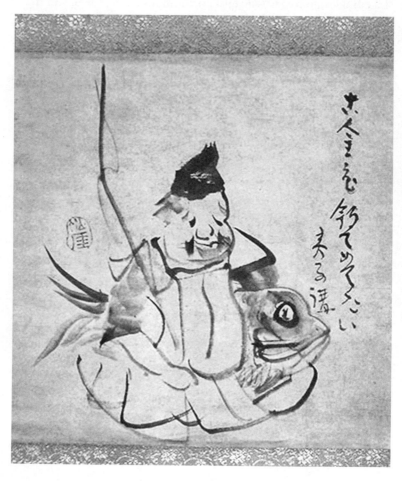

Portrait of "Gold Coin Ebisu" by Sengai Gibon

CHAPTER FIVE

HANAZONO'S ZEN MASTERS

SHUHO MYOCHO [DAITO KOKUSHI]

KANZAN EGEN

Shuho Myocho [Daito Kokushi]

The imperial household had little actual practical power during the Kamakura Shogunate; the Emperor's duties amounted to slightly more than signing official documents and participating in ceremonial religious rituals; however, the Court had more than enough to keep itself occupied with internal wrangling.

A complex system of reigning and "retired" emperors had evolved, initiated by the Emperor Go-Sanjo. Emperors often came to the throne while still children and were then pressured to retire in early youth in order to ensure that they did not acquire any genuine personal power. In the Insei System developed by Go-Sanjo, the "retired" Emperor—who technically entered a monastery and became "cloistered"—was still able to exert influence over his younger successor. The system did not profit Go-Sanjo, as it happened; he died a month after becoming "cloistered."

His son, the Emperor Shirakawa, reigned from 1073 (when he was 20 years old) until 1087, at which time he raised his own son to the throne in order to protect the boy from the machinations of Shirakawa's younger brother who had ambitions of becoming emperor himself. Although Shirakawa became "cloistered," he was able to wield a great deal of influence over his son. This pattern was to be followed by subsequent emperors who, after reigning for a period of time, would retire to a monastery but retain the capacity to exert control over their successors. Some retired and cloistered emperors even maintained their own armies. The situation was further complicated by the fact that, depending upon the longevity of the retired emperors, there could be more than one "Cloistered" Emperor trying to exert influence at any given time. Shirakawa, for example, lived to be 76 years old.

When the Emperor Go-Saga died in 1272, the royal family divided into two branches, both of which claimed the right to determine who sat on the chrysanthemum throne. These branches were made up of the descendants and supporters of Go-Saga's sons, Fukakusa and Kameyama. Fukakusa's branch of the family came to be known as the Jimyoin-to; Kameyama's as Daikakuji-to. Fukakusa became emperor, but the Daikakuji-to did not relinquish their claims. In order to resolve the on-going squabble, the Shogunate determined that the two branches would alternately provide a successor to the throne every ten years.

In 1308, the twelve-year-old son of Emperor Fushimi of the Jimyoin-to line became the Emperor Hanazono. He reigned for ten years, abdicating the throne at age 22 in favor of his second cousin, Go-Daigo of the Daikakuji-to lineage. After abdicating, Hanazono became a "cloistered emperor" not only in name but also in fact, dedicating himself to a serious study of Buddhism.

The retired Emperor heard a rumor that a Zen master of exceptional ability had come to the city of Kyoto where, instead of establishing himself at one of the city's temples, he had chosen to live among the derelicts and beggars residing under the Gojo Bridge. The emperor was intrigued by the tale and asked his informant if there were any way that he could identify which of the beggars was the modest Zen Master. All the informant could tell him was that it was rumored the master was particularly fond of honeydew melons.

Hanazono disguised himself as a fruit peddler and pushed a cart laden with melons to the region by the bridge. As the residents gathered around him, he held up a ripe melon and announced, "I will give this melon freely to anyone who can come up to me and claim it without using his feet."

One of the beggars immediately challenged him, "Then give it to me without using your hands."

It was as much the gleam in the eye of the beggar as his reply that told Hanazono that he had found the Zen teacher he was seeking. His name was Shuho Myocho. He would later come to be known as Daito [Great Light] Kokushi [National Teacher].

When Shuho was only ten years old, he became weary of the things of childhood and turned to serious studies. He sought a teacher to introduce him to the doctrines of Buddhism and began to practice meditation. He was only slightly older when he went on a pilgrimage to various monasteries and hermitages in Japan. While residing at a monastery in Kamakura, he had an initial awakening which deepened his resolve to come to full enlightenment.

Around 1304, Shuho came to Kyoto where he was accepted as a student of Nampo Jomyo (whose posthumous name—Daio Kokushi—is easily confused with Shuho's). Nampo assigned the young man the koan known as Ummon's "*Kan!*" The full koan consists of the replies of three students to a question posed by Suigan Reisan [Cuiyan Lingcan]. Suigen had been head monk under Seppo Gison [Xuefeng Yicun] at the time Ummon [Yunmen Wenyan] was also a student of Seppo [Cf. *Zen Master's of China*, Chapter Nineteen]. Suigen had given the encouragement talks during a meditation retreat, and, once the sesshin was over, he asked three of the participants, "Long have I lectured you these past days. Now, tell me, has Suigan any eyebrows?"

The first monk replied, "A thief surely knows in his heart that he is a thief."

The second monk said, "Rather than falling out from all that talking, they have grown longer!"

And Ummon simply shouted, "*Kan!*" [literally, "barrier" or "gate" as at a border crossing].

After concentrating on "*Kan!*" for ten days, Shuho came to a deep awakening. He later wrote that in penetrating the koan he came to a state of non-duality in which all opposites were reconciled; the whole of the Dharma, he declared, was clear to him. Bathed in sweat, he rushed to express his understanding to his teacher. But before he had a chance to speak, Nampo was able to tell from his deportment that he had attained enlightenment.

"I had a dream last night," Nampo told him, "in which it seemed that the great Ummon himself had come into my room. And here today you are—a second Ummon!"

Shuho, embarrassed by the compliment, covered his ears and fled from his teacher's chamber. But the next day he returned and presented Nampo with two poems he had written to commemorate his achievement:

> Having once penetrated the cloud barrier [*kan*],
> The living road opens out north, east,
>   south, and west.
> In the evening resting, in the morning roaming,
>   neither host nor guest.
> At every step the pure wind rises.

> Having penetrated the cloud barrier [*kan*],
>   there is no old road,
> The azure heaven and the bright sun,
>   these are my native place.
> The wheel of free activity constantly
>   changing is difficult to reach.
> Even the golden-hued monk [Kasyapa]
>   bows respectfully and returns. (18)

Kasyapa, or Mahakasyapa, was the monk to whom the Buddha, in the legendary Flower Sermon, had first passed on the enlightenment tradition. The story is told in the Prologue of *Zen Masters of China*.

Nampo recognized Shuho as his heir and expressed confidence that now his teaching would persist. He then advised the younger man to refrain from taking students for another twenty years; instead, he should use the time to continue his meditation and deepen his understanding. When Nampo died, Shuho left the monastery and spent the next twenty years residing among the indigent, beggars, and street people in Kyoto until the Emperor Hanazono found him under the bridge at Gojo.

Shuho, who in addition to being a master of meditation was also a talented poet and calligrapher, described this time of homelessness in verse:

> Sitting in meditation
> one sees people
> crossing and re-crossing the bridge
> just as they are.

Hanazono eventually became Shuho's disciple, but first it was necessary for the two to acquire an understanding of their relative status. On one occasion, early in their acquaintance, Shuho was seated with Hanazono. Both were on the same level. Protocol would have had it that under normal circumstances the commoner would be below the Emperor, who would be seated on a raised platform. Hanazono, perhaps to draw Shoho's attention to the honor being paid him, remarked casually, "Is it not wondrous that a Zen master should sit at the same level as an Emperor?"

"Is it not wondrous that an Emperor should sit at the same level as a Zen master," Shuho shot back.

Hanazono donated grounds for a new temple to be called Daito-kuji, and Shuho was installed as its first abbot. Both Hanazono and the reigning emperor, Go-Daigo, attended the dedication ceremony officially opening the temple. Shuho would remain at Daitokuji for the rest of his life except for a period of one hundred days during which he acted as abbot of Nampo Jomyo's temple, Sofukuji.

Shuho taught his students to seek their "original countenance," what the Sixth Patriarch in China had called "one's face before one's parents were born."

—the original countenance that you had before you were born of your mother and father! Before you were born of your mother and father means before your mother and father were born, before heaven was separated from earth, before I took on human form. Your original countenance must be seen. (19)

As with the classical Chinese teachers of the Tang dynasty, Shuho maintained that awakening was central to Buddhist practice. In a document called Daito's Testament, he reminded his students, "You have come here not for food or clothing but for religion. As long as you have a mouth, you will have food; as long as you have a body, you will have clothes. Don't concern yourself with these. Be mindful throughout your waking hours; time flies like an arrow, don't waste it with concern over worldly matters." He went on to tell his disciples that even if they were to become the abbots of wealthy monasteries and received the respect of the laity and nobility, even if they were rigorous in their practice of meditation and ritual activities, but they lacked awakening, they were no more than members of the "tribe of evil spirits." Conversely, if they were poverty stricken, lived in a ramshackle hermitage, and ate only what wild food they gathered in the forests and yet they were awakened, then they would be "one who meets me face to face and repays my kindness."

He established a daily schedule of periods of zazen, sutra recitation, and other activities that rivaled the rigors of Chinese monasteries. However, while the monks in China and India limited themselves to only two meals a day, Shuho accommodated the conditions in Japan and permitted a small evening meal that was referred to as "medicine."

In his instructions to his students, Shuho stressed the importance of proper posture and the traditional cross-legged sitting associated with meditation. However, in his fifties he sustained an injury to his leg that prevented him from assuming these postures. When he was in his final illness, he forced his legs into the lotus posture, breaking his bone [a similar story is told of Ummon]. The injured leg bled and the pain was severe, but he sat calmly and took up a brush to compose his death poem

> I have cut off buddhas and patriarchs;
> The Blown Hair [Sword] is always burnished;
> When the wheel of free activity turns,
> The empty void gnashes its teeth. (20)

After completing the poem, he passed away at the age of fifty-six.

KANZAN EGEN

Under Shuho's tutelage, the cloistered emperor, Hanazono, became a sincere devotee of Zen. He converted a portion of one his
country estates into a temple where he intended to pursue his
practice. He had hoped Shuho would take charge of this new
temple, but the master was in poor health. Instead Shuho recom-
mended that the Emperor appoint Kanzan Egen, a monk who
was then living in a mountain hermitage. Respecting his teacher's
advice, Hanazono brought Kanzan to Kyoto and put him in charge
of the temple, which he called Myoshinji.

In contrast to most of the temples in Kyoto—which vied with
one another in their opulence—and despite the fact that it had been
specifically designed for an emperor, Myoshinji was very modest.
Kanzan himself had few aspirations and lived with great simplicity. The monks at Myoshinji raised their own food in the temple
gardens. To some, the temple would have seemed shoddy—the
buildings were allowed to age without being repaired and the roof,
at times, leaked. But sincere Zen students recognized the purity
of the practice under Kanzan's direction.

Kanzan had begun his Buddhist training in Kamakura, then spent
a short time with Shuho's master, Nampo Jomyo. It was Nampo
who gave Kanzan his Buddhist name, Egen. Shortly after they met,
Nampo died, and Kanzan returned to his home province, where
he lived for a while as a hermit. Twenty years passed before he
chanced to learn that Nampo's heir, Shuho, was teaching at Daitokuji. Although he was now over fifty years old, Kanzan sought
to become Shuho's disciple regardless of the fact that Shuho was
younger than he.

Shuho assigned Kanzan the.same koan that had brought him to enlightenment, Ummon's "*Kan!*" Kanzan worked with the koan for two years before resolving it. When at last he did so, Shuho was so pleased with his attainment that he wrote a poem to commemorate the event:

> Where the road is barred and difficult to pass through,
> Cold could eternally girdle the green mountain peaks.
> Though Ummon's single "*Kan*" has concealed its activity
> The true eye discerns [it] far beyond the myriad
>   mountains. (21)

The document, known as "Kanzan's Inka," remains a Japanese treasure in part because of the quality of Shuho's calligraphy.

As his teacher had advised him, Shuho likewise advised Kanzan not to begin teaching at once but rather to allow time for his understanding to deepen. So Kanzan retreated to the village of Ibuka in a distant mountain region where for the next eight years he worked as a farm laborer during the day and spent his evenings in meditation seated on a stone ledge that jutted from the edge of a high cliff. He lived in this manner until the Emperor Hanazono summoned him to Kyoto to become the abbot of Myoshinji.

Although he was now in his sixties, Kanzan continued to live as frugally at Myoshinji as he had in the mountains. The temple was small and could only accommodate a few monks. The disciples Kanzan did accept were subjected to an exacting training. Comforts were few; robes were mended rather than replaced; the temple was drafty and the roof leaked.

The koan Kanzan most frequently assigned was: "There is no birth-and-death around Kanzan." His teaching manner was similar to that of the Chinese Tang masters—he made free use of his staff and shouting. Not many could withstand the rigors of the training, and there were frequent defections. But those who stayed became the basis of one of the strongest lines in Japanese Rinzai. And among those who did remain with Kanzan was the cloistered Emperor Hanazono.

Kanzan lived to be 83 years old. On the day of his death, he told his disciples, "I ask only this of you. Dedicate yourselves to the Great Matter!" Then he donned his travel clothes and went to stand quietly by a pond near the monastery's front gate. In this manner, he died. His disciples, continuing to respect his austerity and anonymity, did not carry out the usual ceremonies, nor was a tomb constructed for his remains.

Portrait of Muso Soseki

CHAPTER SIX

TEMPLE FOUNDERS

KEIZAN JOKIN

MUSO SOSEKI

The two most significant figures in Japanese Zen at the turn of the 14th century were Keizan Jokin and Muso Soseki. Each founded the temple that would become the primary institution of their schools—Keizan was the founder of the Soto Temple Sojiji, and Muso was the founder of the Rinzai Temple Tenryuji.

KEIZAN JOKIN

In the Soto tradition, Keizan Jokin is held in almost as much esteem as Dogen. They are considered equally important in establishing Soto Zen in Japan, but the two men could not have been more different in character or approach.

Dogen was a forceful personality and, especially in his later years, could be inflexible and harsh. When, for example, the Shogun Tokiyori made a gift of certain lands to Eiheiji, one of Dogen's students, a monk named Genmyo, was entrusted with the task of bringing the deeds to his master. Genmyo was so impressed with the generosity of this gift that he boasted of it to his fellow monks. Dogen rebuked Genmyo for being infatuated with worldly affairs and not only expelled him from the monastery but even had his meditation cushions destroyed so that they would contaminate no future student.

Keizan, on the other hand, was noted for the gentleness of his manner. Whenever he found himself moved to anger, he remembered his mother's devotion to the Bodhisattva of Compassion (Kannon) and his anger was dissipated. (The female Bodhisattva, Kannon, is the Japanese manifestation of the Indian Boshisattva Avalokitesvara, who changed gender as well as name when transported from India.)

Dogen and Keizan complemented one another. Dogen's strict formalism was needed to ground the Soto tradition in Japan; Keizan's warm and inviting personality helped to spread the tradition and make it attractive to laity and religious alike. While Dogen had few disciples, Keizan would have many. Dogen is honored as the First Patriarch of Soto Zen in Japan, but Keizan was given the title "Taiso"—which suggests that he was the Patriarch of Greater Importance.

Keizan was raised in a pious household. The devotion of his mother, Ekan Daishi, to the Bodhisattva Kannon was a major influence on his life. His mother had studied for a while with Dogen at Kenninji and eventually became the abbess of Jojuji. During her pregnancy, she made a vow to the Bodhisattva that if her child was born healthy and safely, she would dedicate him to the Buddha and the Dharma.

Keizan became a novice at Eiheiji at the age of eight, and, when he was twelve, he was ordained a monk by Koun Ejo. After Ejo's death, Keizan became the disciple of Tettsu Gikai. When Keizan was seventeen, Gikai advised him to go on a pilgrimage to the various Buddhist centers in Japan and familiarize himself with all the forms of Buddhism then practiced on the islands. The experience would give Keizan a lasting respect for other forms of the religion. He was introduced to the Rinzai tradition at Tofukuji, where he studied with two of Enni Ben'en's successors, Hakuun Egyo and Tozan Tansho, as well as with Shinchi Kakushin who had brought the *Mumonkan* to Japan.

When his pilgrimage was over, he sought out Gikai at Daijoji, where the teacher had gone after withdrawing as abbot of Eiheiji. Gikai remained committed to Soto practice, but he also made use of the koans more commonly associated with the Rinzai School. He assigned Keizan the case in the *Mumonkan* in which Joshu asked his master, Nansen, "What is the way (Tao)?" To which

Nansen replied, "Ordinary mind is the way." [Cf. *Zen Masters of China*, Chapter Twelve.] During one of their formal interviews, Keizan started to explain his understanding of the koan when Gikai stopped him by slapping his face. With that slap, Keizan came to awakening.

Gikai's rival at Eiheiji, Gian, would also later acknowledge Keizan's enlightenment and officiated at the ceremony in which Keizan took the "Bodhisattva Vows"—a strict code of conduct which senior monks could choose to adopt. Keizan, thus, continued the teaching lines of both Gikai and Gian.

He became the founding abbot of Johanji in Awa province. His gentle and compassionate approach to promulgating the Dharma attracted both lay people and monks, and soon he had a large following.

When Gikai retired in 1303, Keizan became abbot of Daijoji in his place, and, as had Johanji, Daijoji flourished under his guidance. While there, Keizan wrote the *Denkoroku*, in which he cataloged the transmission of the Dharma starting with the Buddha and Mahakashyapa down to the transmission from Dogen to Koun Ejo. He also wrote a treatise on Zen practice, the *Zazen Yojinki*, which continues to be used in the Soto tradition as a basic introduction to meditation.

In that book, he described zazen this way:

> *Zazen* clears the mind immediately and lets one dwell in one's true realm. This is called showing one's original face or revealing the light of one's original state. Body and mind are cast off, apart from whether one is sitting or lying down. Therefore one thinks neither of good nor of evil— transcending both the sacred and the profane, rising above

delusion and enlightenment—and leaves the realm of sentient beings and Buddhas. (22)

In a manner similar to Dogen's *Fukanzazengi*, the *Zazen Yojinki* provides detailed instructions on what is conducive to and what harmful to zazen. Practitioners are advised to choose a place neither too hot nor too cold, neither too dark nor too bright. Specifically they are advised to avoid areas in which prostitutes ply their trade. Keizan suggests that the most appropriate place to practice is a temple in a rural setting where the regular changes in the natural world provide a constant reminder of the law of impermanence.

He reviewed the matters of proper posture and breathing, as had Dogen. But Keizan differed from Dogen in advocating the use of koans, such as *Mu*, when the student found it difficult to remain focused during *shikan taza*. He did, however, agree with Dogen that *shikan taza* was the purest form of zazen. The challenge of *shikan taza* is that there is no object, either the breath or a koan, for the practitioner to focus upon. One must sit alert and conscious, but, on the other hand, the goal is not to empty the mind entirely as other meditation techniques attempt to do. The movement of the mind is one of the things of which the meditator is aware, without allowing the flow of the mind to capture one's attention and carry it off into reflection or day-dreaming. It is a difficult balance, to be alert and yet not to fall into reverie. Although with practice the mind will gradually become quieter, it will never become entirely silent. In the same way that as long as the eye is open, there will be sight, so, as long as one is conscious, there will be thoughts. Keizan described this in a poem:

> Though you find clear waters ranging
> to the vast blue skies of autumn,
> how can that compare
> with the hazy moon on a spring night?
> Some people want it pure white,

> but sweep as you will,
> you cannot empty the mind. (23)

In 1311, he turned Daijoji over to one of his Dharma successors and began a period of expansion, founding a number of monasteries all committed to promulgating the Soto tradition. One of the most significant was the transformation of the Shingon Shogakuji on the Noto Peninsula into a Zen temple now known as Sojiji, which remains the primary Soto temple in Japan to this day.

While remaining faithful to Dogen's focus on monastic meditation, Keizan also realized that if Soto Temples were to be supported by the laity in the communities in which they were located, they would have to be responsive to the spiritual needs of those communities. His temples included both a meditation hall and a ceremonial hall in which ritual activities took place for the benefit of the laity. As well, monks supervised funerals, memorial services, and other rites for the benefit of their congregations.

As a result of Keizan's decisions, Soto Temples flourished throughout rural Japan. This would later, however, have an unintended consequence. As it became necessary to provide large numbers of priests to serve these temples, Soto training necessarily became less rigorous. It was not always possible to provide fully awakened teachers for each of these, often very small, temples. So while people still came to Soto monasteries to seek awakening, there were also many who simply wanted authorization to provide religious services for their communities. For those priests, meditation was performed as a devotional activity but rarely did it result in *kensho*.

When Keizan died in 1325, he left behind a school that was vigorous and growing and would come to be the largest within Japanese Zen. After his death, he was given the posthumous name Josai Daishi and the title "Taiso"—Great Master.

MUSO SOSEKI

It is rare that an individual should come to awakening while not under the direction of a teacher and then have that awakening verified. The Chinese Sixth Patriarch was one such example, as was Kyogen Chikan [Xiangyan Zhixian; cf. *Zen Masters of China*, Chapter Fourteen]; so too was Muso Soseki. Because of his own experience, Muso recognized that awakening could just as easily be attained in Japan as in China. There was no need for seekers to go somewhere special in order to achieve enlightenment, and consequently he discouraged those disciples who felt they needed to travel to the Land of Song to deepen their practice.

Muso was born in the nobility, a distant relative of the imperial family. His mother died when he was four years old, and, as was common with children of the nobility, he was placed in a Shingon monastery to be educated. He had an academic nature and enjoyed studying the doctrines and rituals of the Shingon and Tendai Schools.

Although he had been too young to be significantly affected by his mother's death, at eighteen he was very deeply moved by that of one of his teachers. After observing the difficult and painful death of that teacher, Muso found that the issues of religion that he had been studying were no longer abstract. He had been directly confronted with the issue of the frailty of life. He prepared a hermitage and determined to do a 100-day silent retreat in the hope that through meditation he might gain insight into these issues. Before he completed the 100 days, he had a dream in which two famous Chinese Zen monks of the Tang Dynasty appeared to him—Sozan Konin (Sushan Kuangren) and Sekito Kisen (Shitou Xiqian). They presented him with a portrait of Bodhidharma and instructed him to safeguard it.

This dream left such a powerful impression upon him that he took the first characters of the names of the two Zen masters ("So" and "Seki") and combined them to form the name "Soseki," by which he was known for the remainder of his life. This dream, he believed, was a call from his "true nature" to follow the path of Zen. He left his retreat and set out for Shinchi Kakushin's temple on the southern peninsula of the island of Honshu.

Along his journey he stopped at a number of Zen Centers, including that of Issan Ichinei [Yishan Yining], a Chinese Zen master who taught in Kamakura. Issan was concerned that his students be well grounded in Chinese Zen theory and much of his teaching was in the form of lectures. Muso himself would later want to make certain his own disciples had an understanding of the basic tenets of Buddhist doctrine, and he would assert that to preach about the sutras was to preach Zen. But as a young man, he found Issan's approach too abstract for his needs. He lamented that with Issan he had traded the study of Buddhism for the study of Zen; the content was different, but these were still intellectual structures that only "darkened the mind."

He gave up his intention to go to Shinchi and chose to meditate on his own, without a teacher, demonstrating his life-long tendency towards solitude. In this way, he attained a number of insights into Buddhist doctrine but was astute enough to realize that those insights were not the same thing as awakening.

One spring evening, he was meditating under a tree outside of his hermitage. When it was night, he stood up to return to the hut. It was too dark for him to be able to see, and he reached out to where he thought the hermitage wall should be. There was nothing there, and he stumbled and fell. At that moment, it was as if he had fallen through a "wall of darkness" into light. The "unity of all things" was no longer a concept but rather an achieved experience. Heinrich Dumoulin, the cover of whose volume on the history of Japanese Zen is graced with Muso's portrait, quotes the poem the young man wrote to commemorate his awakening:

> For many years I dug the earth and searched for the
>   blue heaven,
> And how often, how often did my heart grow heavier
>   and heavier.
> One night, in the dark, I took stone and brick,
> And mindlessly struck the bones of the empty heavens. (24)

He traveled to Kamakura and met with the Zen teacher, Koho Kennichi, who authenticated his awakening and presented him with a certificate of *inka*.

All of his life, Soseki would be drawn to solitude, but he acquired so much stature within the Zen community that time and again he was called upon to take on responsibilities at various temples. The Emperor Go-Daigo—who would bestow the title Kokushi on Soseki during his lifetime—directed him to serve as the abbot of Nanzenji in Kyoto. Soseki tried to avoid the appointment, as he had several earlier ones, but this time was unable to do so. Nanzenji was the most prominent Zen temple in the country, and, as its abbot, Soseki became a national figure.

He also served for a time as abbot of Engakuji in Kamakura and founded Zuisenji in the Momijigayatsu Valley.

This was a particularly unstable period in Japanese history. Emperor Go-Daigo—the heir of Emperor Hanazono—with the assistance of Ashikaga Takauji, wrestled power away from the Shogunate of the Hojo family, ending the "Kamakura Period." Go-Daigo then sought to re-establish the political power of the Imperial Household, assigning positions of authority to various members of the nobility. Ashikaga Takauji felt that his contributions to the restoration of the Emperor were inadequately appreciated, and he was angered at being excluded from political power in the new government. Muso was astute enough to see that the Ashikaga were unlikely to accept the current situation, and he forged an alliance with the family and in particular with Takauji.

The samurai classes were restive under Go-Daigo, and when the emperor sought to impose a tax for the purposes of building a new palace, Takauji led a coup that ended the so-called "Kemmu Restoration," which had lasted for only three years. Takauji declared himself Shogun, initiating the Muromachi Period. Go-Daigo fled north from Kyoto and sought refuge in Yoshiro. Takauji raised the Crown Prince Komyo (of the Jimyoin-to line), to the status of a rival emperor to Go-Daigo who was of the Daikakuji-to line, and for the next 60 years (1331 to 1392) there would be two claimants to the Chrysanthemum Throne, one in the north and one in the south.

During the conflict between the Emperor and the Ashikaga family, Muso retired to Rinsenji, out of the way of the storm. While there, he composed the *Rinsen Kakun*, a rule for the monastic life, in which he emphasized the importance of zazen over ritual activity of the type being conducted in Keizan's Soto temples. Soseki advocated that monks spend a minimum of four hours a day in meditation.

As a practitioner within the Rinzai tradition, Muso made use of koans but not exclusively. He saw them as a tool that was not necessarily suited to all monks. He noted that the koan tradition was a relatively new one in Buddhism; the earliest Buddhists had not made use of them. They arose in later generations as the zeal of monks for awakening had lessened and special incentives needed to be devised to spur them on. For him, as for the teachers of Enni Ben'en's day, the power of koan study was its ability to promote the necessary "Great Doubt" needed to bring the student to awakening.

Muso also taught that genuine Zen Practice was not limited to periods of formal meditation. The seventh and eighth steps of the Buddha's Noble Eightfold Path are "Correct Mindfulness" and "Correct Meditation." The Zen practitioner is called to remain "mindful" (aware) not only when meditating but during all other activities of daily life. Muso lists eating, drinking, getting dressed and undressed, chanting, and even going to the toilet as examples of opportunities for mindfulness.

The term Muso uses is *kufu*—in Chinese, *gongfu*, or more popularly in English, *kung-fu*. Although the term is now popularly associated with martial arts, it did not originally have that exclusive meaning. *Kufu* referred to any skill developed through effort and practice; martial arts are examples of *kufu*, but so would be masonry, cooking, metal-craft, diplomacy, and so on. The *kufu* of Zen includes mindfulness throughout one's normal activity, no matter how trivial. Everything one does, therefore, becomes part of one's practice, one's *kufu*. "There is," Muso declares, "no difference between the Dharma [law] of the Buddha and the Dharma of the world."

In 1339, the year Emperor Go-Daigo died, and Muso was appointed abbot of Saihoji, a temple where the discipline of the monks had become slack. Muso was able to revitalize the temple and turned it into a center of Zen training. But his most significant achievement at Saihoji was the construction of a moss garden for which the temple would become famous. If Muso was unable to have the solitude he sought, he then determined to create gardens that captured the feel of his beloved rural hermitages. His skill as a landscape designer is one of the things for which he was most respected during his lifetime.

When he was able to leave Saihoji in the care of others, Muso petitioned Takauji to convert one of the imperial palaces in Kyoto into a Zen temple dedicated to the memory of Go-Daigo. In this way the shogun could atone for any responsibility he had for dividing the country. The palace, which had been built on the site of a 9th century temple, was thus returned to its original state. The restored temple was called Tenryuji—Heavenly Dragon Temple. Here again Muso displayed his genius in designing gardens. His technique was to make the garden, which is an artificial construct, appear as natural as possible. He achieved this goal by incorporating not just plants but also stones and mosses in his gardens. A significant part of the legacy he left behind and for which he is remembered in Japan is the association he established between Zen Temples and gardens. A well-designed garden became an effective tool in developing awareness in the Zen practitioner.

Tenryuji became an extremely wealthy temple. In spite of which, Muso retained a taste for simplicity. The story is told that once he visited Kanzan Egen at Myoshinji and was impressed by the stark simplicity of the smaller temple. Kanzan received Muso in a plain, unadorned room. The temple had nothing that the abbot could serve his guest, so a monk was given a few coins and asked to purchase buns from a nearby shop. Then, because he had no flatware, Kanzan served his guest the buns on the lid of an ink box. Muso remarked that Kanzan's school was destined to take precedence over his own.

Muso Soseki died in the year 1351 at the age of 76. In one of his final sermons, he reminded his students to be ever conscious of impermanence.

> The breath of life eventually takes leave of all of us; whether we are young or old, if we live we must die. The number of the dead grows; the blossoms of the flowers fade; the leaves of the trees fall. Things are like foam in a dream. As fish gather in tiny pools of water, so life moves on as the days pass by. Parents and children, husbands and wives who passed their lives together, do not remain together. What use is high standing or wealth? Red cheeks in the morning, dead bones in the evening. Not to trust in the things of this perishing world but to enter upon the way of Buddha— thus will one stir up the mind that seeks the ways and believes in the exalted Dharma. (25)

"Hotei Awakes" by Sengai Gibon

CHAPTER SEVEN

BASSUI

In the end days of the Kamakura era, a pregnant woman of the samurai class had a dream in which she imagined that the child she was carrying would grow up to become a vicious criminal who would slay both of his parents. Terrified by that possibility, when she felt her labor begin, she went out to a field and gave birth in secret, abandoning the child as soon as it was born. A household servant suspecting something peculiar was going on followed her mistress to the field and rescued the child, bringing it back into the household and raising it herself. The child, who would become one of the most important figures in Japanese Rinzai Zen, is known to history by his Buddhist name, Bassui.

The boy grew up in his father's household, apparently fully aware of his actual parents. Perhaps because of the circumstances of his birth he was a particularly sensitive child, given to precocious reflection on the nature of human existence. His father died when Bassui was only four years old. Three years later a memorial ceremony was carried out during which offerings of rice cakes and fruit were presented according to custom. The boy asked those presiding at the ceremony to whom these offerings were being made. "To your father," he was told.

"But my father is dead and his body has been cremated. He no longer has a form. How can he eat these cakes?"

"He may no longer have a physical body, but his soul will receive these offerings," the priests assured him.

Instead of answering his concerns, the reply only raised further questions in the child's mind: What did the priest mean by a "soul"? Did he, too, have one? If so, what was its nature? These questions became the basis of Bassui's "Great Doubt"—the question or concern that propels an individual to seek a resolution.

Bassui's doubt was intense from an early age. While still a child, he was frightened by the cautionary stories he heard about the torments to which the souls of the wicked were subjected after death. The idea that there was a non-physical part of himself which would survive death was not consoling; rather the boy was terrified by the idea that his soul might be capable of experiencing pain after his body was dead. His questioning continued when he became a youth. What was the nature of the soul? Did it really exist or not? If the soul did not exist, then what was it that animated the body, what was it that saw, heard, and felt? What was it that responded to the question "Who are you?" by answering "I am so-and-so"?

He picked up some religious instruction, and, following it as best he could, he meditated on the questions plaguing him. Eventually—like the Buddha before him—he came to the conclusion that there was "no thing" that could be identified as a soul (this is the traditional Buddhist doctrine of *anatta*). He achieved a degree of awareness of what the Heart Sutra [cf. *Zen Masters of China*, Chapter Eight] calls "emptiness" [*sunyata*]—the Void which underlies all of existence and from which all being and experience arises.

This temporarily resolved his worries, but he remained uncertain whether what he had sensed was the same as the "awakening" or *satori* spoken of in Zen circles. In fact, he later came across a passage in his reading that roused all his old anxieties. Even if the nature of all being is *sunyata*, still, Bassui reasoned, there is something that animates the body, which experiences the world through the senses. If it is not "soul," what, then, is it? The way he posed this question was to ask, "Who is the master?" This became, for him, a natural koan, one not assigned by a teacher but one that came from his own nature or mind. As his later writings would point out, the koan is a variation of the question the Sixth Patriarch had put to General Ming [Cf. *Zen Masters of China*, Chapter

Three]: What is one's face before one's parents were born? What is one's True Nature?

It would be natural for a young man, tormented by the issues that obsessed Bassui, to be drawn to enter one of the monasteries then common throughout Japan. The form of Buddhism with which his family was most familiar was Rinzai Zen, which had been adopted as the semi-official religion of the samurai class. The national leadership in Kamakura and later (after the Ashikaga returned the capital there) in Kyoto, were patrons of the Rinzai tradition, and it became the form of Zen favored by the upper classes. By contrast, Soto Zen was more popular with the peasantry and working classes.

Official support of the Rinzai tradition perhaps had more negative consequences than positive ones. Since Rinzai temples had become schools for the sons of the nobility and the warrior class, the government had an interest in how they were organized. When these temples and their abbots gained too much political influence, the Hojo Shogunate took steps to mitigate that power by imposing a system of rules to govern them and setting up an administrative structure known as the *Gozan* or Five Mountain system. It was modeled after a system established in China, where Zen Temples actually had been located in and named after mountains. The government assigned certain temples priority and designated them as the Gozan; five were identified in Kamakura and, under the Ashikaga, another five identified in Kyoto; eventually the Kamakura Temples would become subservient to those in Kyoto. Beneath these chief temples there were ten mid-level establishments (called *jissetsu*) and then a national network of lesser, *shozan*, temples. Muso Soseki had played an active role in developing the Gozan structure and extending it throughout Japan.

Once established, the system inevitably led to greater interference in the operation of those temples. The government approved abbots and controlled the curriculum. Gozan schools became training grounds for students intending to enter the civil service, and they became a vehicle for promulgating government policies in remote districts. As they became centers of growing cultural importance, they lost something of their credibility as spiritual centers. Students with no religious interest at all were sent to them in order to acquire basic literacy skills. Other students were drawn by an interest in various arts that were becoming associated with Zen. Meanwhile, koan study deteriorated from being a powerful and challenging spiritual exercise to becoming a popular literary activity.

Young Bassui was well aware of these conditions and throughout his life distanced himself from the official Rinzai Temple tradition.

At the age of 20, he entered Jifukuji where he sought instruction from a master named Oko. Under Oko's instruction, he began a rigorous meditation practice. However, he still questioned the value of the many ritual activities carried out in the temple and resented the time they took away from zazen. As a consequence, he resisted taking the precepts, choosing instead to practice as a layman. He did so for nine years before finally having his head shaved and becoming a monk. Even then, despite his official change of status, he remained uncomfortable with the trappings of monastic life and remained noncompliant in many regards. He refused to chant sutras or take part in rituals; he even decided not to wear the traditional robes of a monk. He was convinced that the path to awakening could only be found through unstinting meditation. Eventually he even ceased to stay at the monastery and began a pattern he would follow for most of the remainder of his life by choosing to live in a nearby hermitage.

When he decided that Oko could not assist him any further, he began a long tour of other temples. During his time at Jifukuji, he had heard about a hermit named Tokukei Jisha who lived in a small hut in the wilderness. As it happened, both Bassui and Tokukei came from the same village. Intrigued by what he had been told, Bassui sought the hermit out. At their first meeting, Tokukei was confounded by the young man's appearance and re-marked, "I can tell by your shaved head that you are a monk. Why then aren't you wearing the robes of a monk?"

"I became a monk to learn the Buddha way, not to wear special clothing," Bassui answered.

"So do you study the koans of the old masters?"

"Of what use to me are the koans of the old masters when I do not yet understand my own mind?"

"What, then, is your practice?"

"I seek to attain enlightenment for the benefit of all beings in order to help them overcoming their sufferings even if by doing so I should fall into the deepest hells."

Tokukei was so impressed by this answer that he bowed to the youth.

A deep friendship developed between the two who both pre-ferred to live in unassuming hermitages rather than in the increas-ingly wealthy Rinzai monasteries.

No doubt in their discussions Bassui and Tokukei talked about the current status of Buddhism in Japan. They were aware that there were many unqualified teachers at large. Tokukei had never been able to find a teacher in whom he had enough confidence to work with, so he had pursued his own path. Bassui made a determination that he would refrain from teaching until he not only came to full awakening but had that awakening officially confirmed by an appropriate teacher.

He continued to travel throughout Japan, visiting monasteries and speaking with teachers, but never staying within the temple compounds. In the evening, he would withdraw and find an appropriate place to continue his meditations in the countryside, often throughout the night. One morning, after having sat in zazen all night long, he became conscious of the sound of the water flowing in a nearby stream. That experience triggered an initial *kensho*. He proceeded onto Kamakura to meet with Master Kozan Mongo at Kenchoji and asked to be tested. However, even though Kozan confirmed the authenticity of Bassui's attainment, something within Bassui remained dissatisfied and uncertain.

He resumed his pilgrimage of Rinzai centers, testing his understanding of the Dharma with the teachers he encountered. Almost all of the teachers with whom he spoke assured him of the validity of his awakening. Then his friend, Tokukei, told him about Koho Kakumyo, a gifted teacher who was the Dharma heir of Shinchi Kakushin but who had also studied for a time with Keizan Jokin of the Soto tradition. Bassui sought out Koho and at last found a teacher who was not so quick to recognize his awakening. Here, Bassui decided, was a teacher whose guidance would be worth having. As was his habit, Bassui chose to remain in a hermitage outside the temple compound, but he made daily visits to meet with Koho.

These face-to-face meeting with a teacher are known as *sanzen* in the Rinzai Tradition (*dokusan* in the Soto Tradition). During them, the teacher challenges the students and tests his insight. The Chinese Zen Master, Kyogen Chikan [Xiangyan Zhixian] compared the process with the hatching of an egg. Most of the work is done by the chick within the shell, seeking to peck its way out, but, if conditions are appropriate, the mother hen can assist by pecking at the outside of the shell. [Cf. *Zen Masters of China*, Chapter Five]

During one of these meetings, Koho asked his student, "What is your understanding of Joshu's Mu?"

"Mountains, rivers, grasslands, and forests all equally manifest *Mu*."

"That answer still demonstrates self-consciousness," Koho snapped back.

That remark provided the assistance Bassui had needed. He was flooded with understanding and became so overwhelmed he was unable to speak. He recognized the shallowness of his previous insights. He stood and stumbled back to his hermitage, bumping his head as he groped his way to the Temple Gate. Once back in his hermitage, he sat overcome with emotion, weeping freely. The next morning, he returned to see Koho, intending to describe his experience of the night before, but, before Bassui could speak, Koho recognized his attainment and shouted, "My teaching will not vanish!"

Koho carried out the official transmission ceremony, confirming *inka* on the student and giving him the Buddhist name "Bassui" which means "well above average."

Although for the remainder of his life Bassui would consider Koho his master in the Dharma and his most important teacher, in fact he only remained with Koho a few months before resuming his travels. He stopped for a time with Tokukei, to whom he described his time with Koho. Tokukei congratulated him on his good fortune in finding such a teacher and lamented that he had not had a similar opportunity to work with a teacher of Koho's stature. He also warned Bassui of the dangers of remaining too isolated from others, admitting that his own preference for solitude was due in part to pride.

Bassui, however, was still not ready to attach himself to a monastery. He continued his tour of temples, seeking to deepen his awakening through "Dharma Combat" with their teachers. Through these encounters, Bassui began to acquire a reputation, and students started to seek him out although he still doubted that he had attained sufficient insight to be able to assume the responsibility of teaching others. Whenever the number of would-be students became too great or importunate, he would move to another location in order to escape them.

It was not until he was 50 years old that he felt ready to finally accept students. At that time he was living in a mountain village in Yamanashi Prefecture. This time when students gathered around him, he did not flee as in the past. As his fame increased and the number of students increased, the local governor donated land for a temple to be built to accommodate all of them. Bassui, with modesty but without accuracy, called it Kogakuan, rather than Kogakuji, the suffix "an" suggesting a modest hermitage as opposed to "ji" which traditionally meant a temple or monastery. The reality was that Kogakuan was much more than a hermitage; in his later years, Bassui was estimated to have had as many as a thousand disciples, both lay and ordained monks, resident there.

Bassui's teaching was grounded in his own experience and the questions—the "doubt"—that had driven him. A sense of the instruction he gave his students can be had from a letter he wrote to a dying man:

> The essence of your mind is not born, so it will never die. It is not an existence, which is perishable. It is not an emptiness, which is a mere void. It has neither color nor form. It enjoys no pleasures and suffers no pains.
>
> I know you are very ill. Like a good Zen student, you are facing that sickness squarely. You may not know exactly who is suffering, but question yourself: What is the essence of this mind? Think only of this. You will need no more. Covet nothing. Your end, which is endless, is as a snowflake dissolving in the pure air. (26)

On another occasion, he said:

> Those who wish to break the cycle of rebirth must know the way of becoming a Buddha. The way of becoming a Buddha is the way of enlightenment. Before one's father and mother were born and before one's own body was formed, one's mind existed unchanged until now, as the ground of all sentient beings. This is also called one's original countenance. This mind is pure from the beginning. When the body is born, it is without the form of life, and when the body dies, it is without the form of death. Neither does it have the form of man or woman, of good or evil. Because there is nothing to which it can be compared, it is called Buddha nature. From this mind there arise ten

thousand images, like waves on a vast great sea or forms reflected in a mirror. (27)

The passage above comes from a collection of his sayings compiled by one of his students, a disciple named Myodo. Myodo also included a biography of his teacher and a number of anecdotes. When he had completed the manuscript, he brought it to Bassui and asked him to suggest an appropriate title for the work. Bassui was surprised to learn of Myodo's efforts and told him, "This is your doing, not mine. What name should I suggest for such a mixture of mud and water?" So the volume came to be known as *Mud and Water* (*Wadeigassui*).

In 1387, at the age of 61, Bassui was seated in zazen with a group of his disciples. He suddenly shouted at them: "Look directly! What is this? Look and you will not be deceived!" He repeated the words a second time, then passed away.

Portrait of Ikkyu Sojun

CHAPTER EIGHT

IKKYU SOJUN

Ikkyu Sojun is such a popular figure in Japanese folk culture that he became the subject of a televised cartoon series. He achieved fame not only for his prowess as a Zen Master but for his poetry, calligraphy, heterodoxy, and libido.

Legend has it that he was the illegitimate son of Emperor Go-Komatsu, who reunited the Northern and Southern courts in 1392. When Ikkyu's mother became pregnant, she was banished from the court by the Empress and fled to the southern island of Kyushu, where she raised her child in poverty. The circumstances of his childhood and his mother's difficulties were formative influences in Ikkyu's life. From them he acquired a life-long aversion to the upper classes and a sympathy for working people, in particular for the tribulations of the women of that era and culture.

When he was five years old, his mother became fearful for his safety. Worried that competing political factions might seek him out and attempt to use the Emperor's illegitimate child for their own purposes, she enrolled her son in Ankokuji, a Rinzai Temple of the Gozan System. The boy proved to be a precocious student and demonstrated an early proclivity for poetry, calligraphy, and mischief.

A popular tale relates how one day, while he was still very young, he happened accidentally to break an antique teacup which was a particular favorite of the abbot's. Ikkyu concealed the shards in the sleeves of his robe and went to see the abbot.

"Sir," he inquired disingenuously, "why is it that people die?"

"This is the way of nature," the abbot told him, a little pompously. "When conditions are appropriate, things are born, and, when other conditions are appropriate, things pass away."

"Well then," the boy said, revealing the broken pieces of the heirloom, "it looks like the conditions were appropriate for your teacup to pass away."

Even as a youth, Ikkyu had a naturally reflective temperament. He was drawn to Buddhist practice, but he was also sensitive to the discrepancy he observed between the way monks lived in the temple and the principles of monastic life to which they paid lip service. He was also discouraged by the deference students and teachers alike paid to certain monks not because of their spiritual attainments but because of their social rank.

By the time of the Ashikaga Shogunate, Zen had become as much a cultural phenomenon as a religious one, and, as the cultural and artistic components became more dominant in certain temples, there was a corresponding attenuation of the spiritual teaching. At Ankokuji, Ikkyu received a good literary education, which would serve him well in later life, but he realized that if he wished to achieve enlightenment he would need to seek a teacher elsewhere.

Not far away lived a hermit named Keno Soi. Ikkyu was drawn to the hermit because of his simple lifestyle and apparent sincerity of purpose. Keno, however, was not a transmitted teacher and admitted to Ikkyu that he was uncertain how much help he could be. Ikkyu had received some training in zazen at Ankokuji, but his experience of meditation under Keno's guidance was very different. Neither Ikkyu nor Keno, however, knew whether this was evidence of awakening or was rather only an experience of *samadhi*—the deep state of absorption that often precedes kensho.

Ikkyu worked with Keno until the latter's death, five years later. He was so distressed by his teacher's passing that he attempted to drown himself. A passerby rescued him, but he remained despondent for a long while.

Eventually he decided to apply to be accepted as a student of Kaso Sodon, reputed to be one of the most demanding Zen Masters of his time. Kaso was abbot of Daitokuji, the prestigious monastery established by Daito Kokushi. Daitokuji was a *rinka* temple—the term applied to temples outside of the Gozan System. The majority of these were rural and Soto; Daitokuji, located within Kyoto, was the most significant Rinzai rinka temple. Without neglecting his duties as abbot, Kaso had given up his quarters in Daitokuji and chose to live in a hermitage in the village of Katata, on the shore of Lake Biwa. There he worked with a small, select group of students.

When Ikkyu first presented himself at the hermitage, Kaso—following a tradition that went back to Bodhidharma and Eka—barred the door and refused to receive him. Ikkyu persisted, sitting outside the hermitage in meditation posture and sleeping under an upturned boat at night. For five days, Kaso gave Ikkyu no encouragement and even, on one occasion, tried to chase him off by having his disciples drench him with water, but Ikkyu did not waver. Finally, convinced of the supplicant's sincerity, Kaso relented and accepted Ikkyu as a student.

Kaso assigned Ikkyu the fifteenth case in the *Mumonkan*. The incident described took place during the initial meeting between Tozan Shusho [Ch: Dongshan Shouchu] and his teacher, Ummon Bun'en [Yunmen Wenyan—cf. *Zen Masters of China*, Chapter Nineteen]. Ummon asked the younger man where he had come from. Tozan named his home province.

"And where did you spend the summer?" Ummon asked.

Tozan named the monastery beside the lake.

"When did you leave the monastery?"

"On the twenty-fifth of August."

"I spare you thirty blows."

Ikkyu worked on this koan for three years. In addition to his regular sittings with the other monks, Ikkyu spent his evenings meditating in a small fishing boat floating on the lake. Finally, while listening to a group of singers who were performing at the temple, Ikkyu had an initial, but relatively shallow, awakening experience. Kaso recognized the validity of the experience and gave the young man his Buddhist name in recognition of his achievement, but he also told Ikkyu that he had only a "tongue-tip taste" of Zen and directed him to continue to work on the koan.

An initial kensho does not necessarily bring about full satori—or awakening. Although with kensho the way in which the Zen practitioner sees things undergoes a radical change, there is often room for further growth. Kensho brings about a qualitative change in the practitioner's perception; the opportunity for quantitative deepening of that perception persists long past the initial experience. The 20th century Japanese teacher, Yasutani Kakuun, made this comparison: If one were in a windowless room in which there was no light whatsoever and one lit a match, that would bring about a qualitative difference in one's situation. Previously there had been no light, now there was a slight light. If the person then used the match to light a candle, used the candle to find a flashlight, and finally used the flashlight to locate the light switch, each of those would be quantitative changes.

Undiscouraged, Ikkyu continued to focus on his koan for another two years. Then, while he was meditating in the boat on Lake Biwa, the loud call of a crow startled him into full awakening. This experience was so profound that Ikkyu had no doubt of its validity and considered not bothering to have it authenticated. On reflection the next morning, however, he decided to abide by the usual protocol and present his understanding to Kaso.

Kaso listened to Ikkyu, then made a dismissive gesture. He compared Ikkyu to one of the early followers of the Buddha, the *arhats*, who may have thought they were enlightened but had not yet reached the level of understanding expected within the Zen tradition. "This is still only the level of understanding of a beginner," he said. "You are nowhere near the level of a Master yet."

"Then I am content to remain a beginner," Ikkyu told him.

"Ah, then you have reached the level of a Master after all."
Ikkyu commemorated his awakening in a poem:

Violent wrath and passions linger in my heart
For twenty years which is this moment.
A crow laughs, as an arhat from this dusty world.
What means the beautiful face singing in the sunshine? (28)

It is said that when Kaso presented Ikkyu with the formal certificate of Dharma transmission, the younger man threw the document on the fire. The document was retrieved, but at various times in his career Ikkyu threatened to destroy it. At one point, his disciples had to rescue the pieces of the torn document and paste them together. Ikkyu was leery of the formal customs associated with the established Zen tradition. He refused to give his own students certificates of *inka* since such documents could now be purchased from less scrupulous teachers and, to his mind, were no longer credible evidence of a practitioner's level of attainment. Although Kaso was equally concerned about the formal structures of the Rinzai School, Ikkyu's flouting of convention was a matter of tension between the two of them.

After awakening, Ikkyu remained with Kaso until the latter's death, but their relationship was not always an easy one. Kaso strictly adhered to the Buddhist principles and the monastic code of conduct, whereas Ikkyu had amorous affairs, dallied with prostitutes, and was fond of saki. On one occasion, Kaso had to chide Ikkyu for not showing appropriate deference to distinguished visitors who came to the monastery.

For his part, Ikkyu remained devoted to his teacher. In his last years, Kaso became physically incapacitated, and Ikkyu acted as his personal attendant, carrying him from place to place when necessary, even helping him when he used the privy. But when it was time for Kaso to acknowledge an heir, he chose a more traditional monk, Yoso, as his successor.

Ikkyu was in his early thirties when Kaso died. He did not have a great deal of respect for Yoso, who he considered to be little more than an administrator, so he left Daitokuji. He was officially qualified to teach but chose not to. Instead he adopted the life of an itinerant monk, moving between the cities of Kyoto and Osaka, visiting wine shops and brothels as often as he did Zen Temples. He even suggested in his poetry that the time spent with prostitutes was as significant as his enlightenment experience. In one poem, he wrote that the caw of the crow was fine, but the night he had spent with a pretty prostitute "opened a wisdom deeper than what that bird said." (29)

Although Yoso and Ikkyu did not get along well, Yoso recognized Ikkyu's attainment and invited him to return to Daitokuji and assume responsibility for one of the sub-temples in the compound. Ikkyu only spent ten days in the role before deciding that temple administration and the endless round of ceremonies he was expected to carry out had little to do with Zen. He wrote a parting poem and resumed his travels:

> I've spent ten days in this temple, my mind awhirl
> Entangled in formalities which never stop
> If anyone wants to find me now
> Try the fish stand, brothel, or wine shop.

Ikkyu was as critical of the pretentions of monks who affected a sanctimonious lifestyle as he was of the ritualism of the temples. In both cases, the practitioners were cut off from the realities of ordinary life. He was fond of referring to a story found in the collection of koans known as *Shumon Kattoshu* [*Entangled Vines*]. It told of a pious widow who had built a hermitage for a Zen monk and supported him for twenty-some years. One day she became curious about the level of understanding the monk had acquired during this time. To test him, she enlisted the aid of a young girl.

"Visit this monk I've been supporting," she said, "put your arms around him, rub up against him a bit, and let him know you're willing to do whatever he'd like. Then come and tell me how he responds."

The girl was naturally flirtatious and not at all averse to testing the old monk. She went into his hut dressed in her best kimono and knelt down beside him as he sat, sternly, in meditation. She massaged his shoulders and pressed her breasts into his back. "What would you like to do now?" she whispered in his ear.

"In winter, an old tree grows from a barren rock," the monk said, sententiously. "There's no warmth to be found anywhere."

The girl had no idea what the monk meant, but she returned to the old woman and reported what had taken place.

"What a charlatan!" the old woman exclaimed.

"Do you think he should have made love to me?" the girl asked.

"Not necessarily, but he should have shown sympathy for your condition and spoken to you about it. He demonstrated no compassion whatsoever. I've wasted the money I've spent on that rascal all these years."

Then she turned the monk out of the hermitage and burned it to the ground.

Ikkyu wrote a verse commentary to the tale in which is commended the old woman's generosity in providing a young bride for the monk. He added:

If I had been offered something similar,
That old tree would have put forth new green shoots.

Stories about Ikkyu's travels circulated even during his lifetime. There is a story, for example, about an occasion when he was practicing *takahatsu*—the monastic tradition of begging for food. He came to the house of a wealthy landowner who, although he professed to be a Buddhist, gave Ikkyu only a single small coin and that grudgingly. Ikkyu returned to his dwelling and put on the formal robes of a transmitted Zen Master; wearing these, he returned to the landowner's house. The landowner eagerly invited Ikkyu in and ordered an elaborate meal prepared for his guest. When the meal was served, Ikkyu stood, took off his robes and placed them on the seat of honor.

"This meal has obviously been prepared not for me but for my clothes," he remarked. Then he left the house.

In another tale, Ikkyu was crossing Osaka Bay on a ferry when a warrior monk of the Yamabushi School approached him. Yamabushi combined Shingon and Tendai teachings with native Shintoism; its adherents were trained in martial arts and magic.

"You're a Zen monk, aren't you?" the warrior monk asked.

Ikkyu admitted he was.

"I've heard that your school produces great meditators, but what else can you do?"

"I don't know. What can you do?"

"We're trained to be warriors and magicians. We can perform miracles which terrify our enemies and amaze the people, and, by doing so, we bring many to respect the Buddha way. Can you do anything like that?"

"Certainly there are miracles in the Zen tradition, but tell me what kind of miracles you can do."

"I can call up the Bodhisattva Fudo on this very boat." Fudo was a guardian bodhisattva usually portrayed bearing a sword and a rope and surrounded by a fiery halo.

"That would be impressive," Ikkyu admitted. "Please show me."

The monk began a series of chants and prayers and then, indeed, the Bodhisattva appeared in the boat surrounded by his halo of flames. The other passengers fell to their knees in amazement.

"Can the Zen monk match my skill?" the Yamabushi asked.

"Well, I'm capable of a miracle or two as well," Ikkyu said. "For example, I can make water with my own body." So saying, he pulled out his penis and urinated on the flames surrounding the bodhisattva, putting them out.

Ikkyu was a calligrapher, a poet, and a musician. Some of his poems dealt with topics one would expect from a Zen Master. These two renditions are by Stephen Addis:

> Originally nonexistent
> your long-ago self
> will go nowhere at death—
> for there's nowhere to go
> and nothing at all (30)

In this world
we eat, we shit
we sleep and we wake up—
and after all that
all we have to do is die (31)

On a similar theme:

Once born
we are all destined to die
even Buddha Shakyamuni
even Bodhidharma
even cats and kitchen ware

Other poems are not only secular, several were sexually explicit,
many of these celebrating his relationship with a blind musician
named Mori with whom he became involved in later life. In one
of his best known poems, Ikkyu compares his hand with Mori's,
then goes on to praise her erotic skills, remarking that when he was
ill, she was able to enliven his "jade stalk," much to the happiness
of his disciples.

In another he rejoices in the vigor this much younger woman
roused in him:

white-haired priest in his eighties
Ikkyu still sings aloud each night to himself to the sky
   the clouds

because she gave herself freely
her hands her mouth her breasts her long moist thighs (32)

When he was in his 60s, Ikkyu settled at Myoshoji, the small temple that had been built to honor the memory of Daito Kokushi. Here at last he gathered a few students. The situation at Myoshoji suited him. It did not bring with it much public attention, and the number of students with whom he worked was never large.

His situation underwent a dramatic change, however, during the Onin Wars over who would be the successor to the shogun, Ashikaga Yoshimasa. During the fighting, which lasted for ten years and devastated much of the country, many temples, including Daitokuji, were destroyed. Ikkyu felt obligated to return there and spent the last years of his life struggling to rebuild it. He was able to raise the funds necessary for the reconstruction and reluctantly assumed the official position of abbot, but he was not happy with his new situation. He expressed his feelings in a short poem; the purple robes he refers to those are those of an abbot.

Thirty years a vagrant and a wanderer
Now humiliated by purple robes

As the abbot of a major temple, he drew a larger number of students, and, in spite of the fact that he was celebrated in popular culture for his unorthodox lifestyle, he proved to be an effective and demanding teacher. He made use of the traditional koan collections, but he also stressed the importance of maintaining one's practice under all circumstances. He taught that the mindfulness one applied during meditation to the breath or to the gnawing question of the koan should be applied to all the other aspects of one's life.

> Don't pick up tea leaves, but practice zazen.
> Don't read sutras, but practice zazen.
> Don't clean the house, but practice zazen.
> Don't ride on horseback, but practice zazen.
> Don't make fermented beans, but practice zazen.
> Don't sow tea seeds, but practice zazen. (33)

One of the most frequently told stories about Ikkyu relates his response to a layman who approached him while he was abbot of Daitokuji.

"Master, you are renowned both for your wisdom and the beauty of your calligraphy," the layman said. "It would be a great honor if you would write down some words of guidance which I could hang on my wall and reflect upon."

Ikkyu took up his writing brush and, with a flourish, wrote the single word "Attention" on a piece of paper.

"'Attention?'" the layman read. "Could you elaborate?"

Ikkyu wrote a second time, "Attention."

"That's not much," the layman protested, uncertain whether his request were being taken seriously or not.

Ikkyu wrote one more time, "Attention."

"Okay, okay," the layman spluttered. "But what does 'attention' mean?"

"Attention," Ikkyu told him, "means Attention."

Even while at Daitokuji, Ikkyu continued to flaunt his lack of convention. He maintained his relationship with Mori. The two could be heard in the evenings playing duets. She was a harpist and vocalist, and he accompanied her on the flute.

As he felt his death approaching, at age eighty-seven, he wrote a final, characteristically irreverent poem:

> age eighty weak
> I shit and offer it to Buddha (34)

Ink splash painting by Sesshu Toyo

CHAPTER NINE

ZEN STYLE

SESSHU TOYO

MURATA SHUKO

SOEKI RIKYU

Zen practitioners such as Bassui and Ikkyu distanced themselves from the official structures of the Rinzai School because of what they perceived to be the harmful effect the Gozan System had had upon it. Having acquired official status within the machinery of state, Gozan Temples performed a number of functions in addition to being training grounds for monks. While the sons of the nobility and the warrior classes attended the schools associated with the five major temples, feudal lords outside of Kyoto recruited Zen monks to establish schools at their courts, extending the influence of the Gozan system. Temples could be commercial establishments. Some acted as banks; others were publishing centers, where school texts, along with both Buddhist and Confucian documents from China, were made available in woodcut prints. The temples also carried out ritual activities for the benefit of the national government. In many temples, religious teaching became slack. Monks unable to earn them could purchase documents of enlightenment. Very probably the majority of those enrolling at Gozan temples had no more religious aspiration than parochial school students in North America.

These were some of the negative effects of the Gozan System. There were positive consequences as well.

Regardless of the young person's religious interest, all students were introduced to the practice of zazen. Although it is primarily a spiritual exercise, zazen does not work automatically. It is not a technique for awakening so much as it is a means of putting oneself into a condition where one is susceptible to awakening. The technique, however, does help the practitioner develop other qualities that were discovered to have practical applications outside monastic life. These skills included discipline, concentration, and the cultivation of *mushin*—or "no mind."

Mushin is the state described in the *Heart Sutra* [cf. Chapter Eight of *Zen Masters of China*], the state of the "True Self" or "Original Mind." It is the state Dogen described in his essay, *Genjokoan*, where he wrote: "Studying the Buddha Way is studying oneself. Studying oneself is forgetting oneself. Forgetting oneself is being enlightened by all things." Through zazen, one's personal ego—what one generally thinks of as one's "self"—is discovered to be an "illusion" in that it is the product of training, habit, and environment. It is the self that analyzes, plots, and plans; those are its strengths and why it is so important. However, it is not usually particularly creative or spontaneous. The "emptiness" which is spoken of in the *Heart Sutra* is, at least in part, to be "empty of ego." It is a state equally familiar to and valuable to artists and athletes. Once one has mastered the mechanics of one's craft or sport, inspiration is often liberated when the ego-self is abrogated; what one cannot do consciously, one may be able to accomplish instinctively. In sport, for example, there is no time for the athlete to think about his or her moves during competition. Likewise, the painter who seeks to achieve an effect through effort will almost inevitably produce a work inferior to one in which the hand moves, as it were, without intention.

Students who had no particular desire to achieve awakening discovered that their practice of zazen helped them in other ways.

The Kyoto temples had become repositories of Chinese artworks brought back to Japan by visiting monks. Paintings like those of Ma Yuan became national treasures and served as models for Japanese artists. (35) Chinese calligraphy was also much admired and imitated.

Students in Gozan schools were introduced to a variety of arts, and, as these arts were further developed, a Zen style began to emerge. Far more so than in China, where there had been older and more powerful influences to compete with, this Zen style permeated Japanese arts and left a lasting impression on the national culture.

Zen masters were themselves often artists of rare merit. Muso Soseki's skill as a landscape designer has already been noted. Since the monasteries outside of Kyoto were often located in isolated rural settings, it was natural for the monks in residence to develop an appreciation of natural beauty. But even in the larger cities, the gardens attached to Zen monasteries were noted for their elegance. The designs ranged from reproductions of wild landscapes to the famous austere raked sand and boulders of *karesansui* gardens such as that at Ryoanji.

Soseki as well as Ikkyu and Dogen were all admired for the quality of their calligraphy. Chinese characters, used in formal Japanese writing, are so expressive in themselves that they lend themselves to calligraphy in a way that the simpler Roman alphabet does not. As a result, calligraphy evolved into a serious art form in both China and Japan.

Calligraphy is known as *shodo* in Japanese—the way (do) of writing. It is done with a brush, rather than a pen, and thick ink. The absorbency of the paper used does not allow for hesitation or correction. The artist's hand needs to move smoothly and with assurance. The writing has to be spontaneous and fluid. One cannot think about what one is doing. *Mushin* is the ideal state for the calligrapher, allowing the work to flow through him or her rather than being consciously carried out.

A story is told of the 19th century Zen master, Imakita Kosen [Chapter Twenty] whose calligraphy was copied and reproduced in wood to grace the entrance gate of Manpukuji in Kyoto. The young student assigned to prepare the ink for Kosen was not shy about expressing his opinion of the master's work. After Kosen's first attempt, the student remarked that the work did not come up to his usual standards. Kosen tried again, and the student noted—accurately—that the second was not even as good as the first. In this manner, Kosen wrote the same characters eighty-four times, none of which met with the student's approval.

Finally Kosen sent the student on an errand and, while the young man was away, the master collected himself and, undistracted by the critical observation of the student, took up his brush for the eight-fifth time. When the student returned, he expressed his sincere admiration for the final effort, which, when in place at Manpukuji, was universally recognized as a masterpiece.

SESSHU TOYO

The same fluidity of style characteristic of the best calligraphy is also required in brush painting. The materials used are the same, and—unlike the oils or acrylics of western artists—do not allow for changes to be made after the ink is on the paper. Calligraphy and painting were often combined.

Painters who received their training in the Gozan Schools naturally chose Zen subjects, such as masters from the past and incidents of Zen history, but, like their Chinese predecessors, they also demonstrated a love of landscape painting and the natural world.

The most celebrated artist of the 15th century—some maintain the greatest Japanese artist of all time—was Sesshu Toyo. As was then common, he was enrolled at a Zen monastery near his home while still a child. His training was both spiritual and secular. A popular tale about his childhood, however, suggests that his inclination was toward the latter. It is related that on one occasion he was tied to a pillar in the meditation hall for some infraction of monastic discipline—possibly for spending more time drawing than meditating. When the allotted time for the punishment had elapsed, a monk came to the hall to release Sesshu and was startled at seeing a rat by the boy's foot. The monk sought to chase it away before it bit the child, only to discover that the rodent had been drawn on the floor mat with ink made from Sesshu's tears mixed with dust.

When Sesshu was twenty, he came to Kyoto to study Zen with Shunrin Suto at Shokokuji, one of the Five Mountain monasteries. His youthful resistance to monastic discipline had been quelled by this time, and he was respected for the sincerity and depth of his Zen practice. He also studied painting under Tensho Shubun, the most respected Japanese painter of the day—although both Tensho's fame and reputation would be eclipsed by those of his student.

When he was forty, Sesshu was appointed Chief Priest at Unkokuji in Yamaguchi. It was from the port of Yamaguchi that many of the ships sailing to China embarked, and, in 1468, Sesshu took part in one of these expeditions. He was commissioned to purchase Chinese works of art, but the trip also gave him an opportunity to study with Chinese masters and to hone his skills, although it is said that when he arrived on the Asian mainland he found the current Ming Dynasty artists to be, in his opinion, inferior to their predecessors. Regardless, during his time in China, his own skill and fame grew.

His adopted name—Sesshu—means Boat of Snow. He acquired it, according to one story, when he was preparing to board the ship that would return him to Japan. A crowd of wellwishers came to see him off and showered him with bits of white paper on which they asked him to paint even a few strokes before leaving.

He returned to Japan to find the capital in ruins from the continuing Onin Wars, so he spent some years traveling about the islands. Eventually, around 1486, he returned to Yamaguchi and dedicated himself to art. His painting was an expression of his

Zen practice. As the Jesuit historian of Zen, Heinrich Dumolin, put it:

> The life and feeling that breathe within Sesshu's paintings of nature are evidence of his Zen spirituality. As the body of Buddha, nature is in a constant process of growth; therefore anyone who seeks present nature from within has to enter into this process. This is precisely what Sesshu sought to do in his ink paintings; he excels all others in his ability to see into the changing seasons and into the exuberance of plant life. (36)

His work was lauded throughout Japan, and he was offered several posts and honors all of which he declined. After his death, his paintings were deemed national treasures. A probably apocryphal story tells of a man who owned one of Sesshu's scrolls. When his house caught fire—as Japanese paper and lath construction was wont to do—he realized he could not escape and that the precious work of art would also be destroyed. So he cut open his abdomen and placed the scroll within his body, where it was later found unharmed in his charred corpse.

MURATA SHUKO

The art in which Zen style is most fully evident is *chanoyu*—the tea ceremony. This evolved from the Chinese monastic practice, carried over to Japan, of serving tea to visitors. The secular ceremony in Japan is traced back to a student of Ikkyu, Murata Shuko, who once declared that the taste of tea and the taste of Zen were the same. Ikkyu taught his disciple that by paying appropriate attention to the homely activity of steeping and serving tea, he could bring the act to sacramental status. This awareness or mindfulness, however, cannot be forced; one cannot be truly aware if one makes an effort to be aware. Therefore, to properly serve tea one needs to be in the same state of mushin as the calligrapher.

The ceremony Shuko developed was both formal and aesthetic. A special teahouse was designed and kept deliberately small. Indoor space was measured by the size of tatami mats, which were slightly less than 3 x 6 feet (1 x 2 meters). A teahouse was traditionally four and a half mats, or approximately 9 foot square. The doorway was low, so that all who entered had to bow in order to do so. The interior space was sparsely decorated, with perhaps a painting or an example of calligraphy on the wall, and a small alcove in which a simple floral arrangement—the predecessor of the art of *ikebana*—was displayed.

Shuko explained the atmosphere he sought to achieve by relating the story of a Chinese poet who had described the vivid contrast between blossoms on a plum tree in early spring against the woods still covered with snow. A friend of the poet suggested the poem would be more effective if only a single flower had bloomed against the white background. The starkness of that contrast is what Shuko achieved by placing just one flower in a vase within the austere tea shed.

D. T. Suzuki described the atmosphere of the tea ceremony in his *Zen and Japanese Culture*:

> The tea-drinking . . . is not just drinking tea, but it is the art of cultivating what might be called "psychosphere," or the psychic atmosphere, or the inner field of consciousness. We may say that it is generated within oneself, while sitting in a small semi-dark room with a low ceiling, irregularly constructed, from handling the tea bowl, which is crudely formed but eloquent with the personality of the maker, and from listening to the sound of boiling water in the iron

kettle over a charcoal fire. Let time pass for a while, and as one feels more composed, one begins to notice another kind of sound coming from outside the windows. It is the water dripping from a bamboo trough that conducts it from somewhere on the mountainside. The dripping is neither scanty nor excessive, it is just enough to lead the mind to a state of tranquil passivity. (37)

The implements are chosen for their beauty as much as for their function. And in this highly stylized environment the tea master prepares and serves the beverage for a group of no more than four guests. Etiquette limits conversation to a discussion of the artistic merits of the wall hanging or the utensils. Affairs of state or other matters were proscribed. The teahouse, thus, became a refuge from daily cares and concerns, and, as such, became popular with both military leaders and the nobility. Shuko, for example, was employed as tea-master to Yoshimasa, the eighth shogun of the Ashikaga Era.

Soeki Rikyu

The most famous tea-man was Soeki Rikyu. He was the son of a fish merchant in the port city of Sakai. It was to this port that highly prized tea implements were imported from China and Korea. So it happened that the fishmonger's son first encountered the tea ceremony as it was prepared for the merchants of the region.

His aesthetic sense was cultivated while he was studying Zen at Daitokuji. On one occasion he was assigned the task of sweeping the courtyard of the temple to prepare for the arrival of an important visitor. The boy was assiduous in clearing the area of every single leaf and stone. When one of the senior monks came to check his work, the monk looked over the area critically. Then he took hold of the branch of a tree and shook it so that a few leaves fluttered down and scattered over the empty space. Rikyu immediately recognized that this improved the appearance of the courtyard.

After he left Daitokuji, Rikyu developed the art of tea to such a degree that he was invited to Kyoto to serve as tea-master for the military leaders Oda Nobunaga and Toyotomi Hideyoshi.

These men found themselves revitalized by taking time to refresh themselves by participation in the tea ceremony. However, not all samurai found the practice appealing.

The story is told of the adjutant to a military commander who studied tea under Rikyu; the adjutant believed that by doing so the commander was demonstrating an inappropriate softness and effeminacy. He decided that in order to save his master's honor he needed to execute the offending tea-man. He came to the teahouse as a patron, but Rikyu was able to discern the warrior's intention merely by looking at him. He invited the man in, asking him to first leave his sword outside. The adjutant asserted that he was a samurai and was never parted from his sword. Rikyu conceded the point and ushered the visitor into the teahouse. The samurai took his place on the mats, laying his sword beside him.

The charcoal fire was prepared and the iron kettle placed over it to come to a boil. Once the water was roiling, Rikyu moved his arm and, as if by accident, tipped the kettle over. Steam filled the small hut, and the young officer rushed outside to escape being scalded.

Rikyu came out and apologized for his clumsiness. Then he invited the adjutant back in for his tea. "I have safely placed your sword here, under the mat," Rikyu told him. "When we are finished, I will clean it off for you and return it."

The younger man realized he had been bested and forsook his design to kill the tea-man.

Although he was not a monk, Rikyu became the subject of many stories that are now part of the Zen tradition. One of the most famous tells of a visit that his patron, Hideyoshi, intended to make to the master's teahouse. Hideyoshi had been told that the morning glories blooming beside it were particularly impressive that year. When he arrived at the teahouse, however, he discovered that Rikyu had cut down all the vines. On entering the small tearoom, Hideyoshi found a single flower placed in a vase. Rikyu, following the example of Shuko, had sacrificed all the morning glories outside for the sake of a single blossom.

Two of the qualities that calligraphy, the tea ceremony, and the other Zen-inspired arts share in common are known as *wabi* and *sabi*. *Wabi* suggests the type of simplicity associated with rustic implements of former times. It implies a state of naturalness, similar to that advocated in Chinese Daoism; to be in a state of *wabi* is to be at home in and intimate with the natural world. *Sabi* also refers to antique times and to a sense of solitude as well as a lack of pretension.

On one occasion, Rikyu and one of his students were visiting another district. There they came upon a teahouse with a beautiful old but decrepit door. The student commented that the door seemed, to him, to have the qualities of *wabi* and *sabi*.

"Not at all," Rikyu corrected him. "Consider the wood of that door. It comes from a tree not native to this region. This door was brought to this teahouse from a great distance and at obvious expense. That is pretention; it is not true *sabi*."

Hideyoshi—like many tyrants—was a deeply paranoid individual. There is also some evidence that he was jealous of Rikyu's acclaim. Whatever the factors, he became suspicious that Rikyu was in some way disloyal to him and condemned the tea-man to die. However, because of their long relationship and the esteem in which Rikyu was generally held, the tea-master was allowed the privilege usually granted only to samurai of ritually disemboweling himself in the act of *seppuku*—vulgarly known as *hara-kiri*.

Rikyu accepted his fate, and, on the appointed day, he invited a choice group of friends and disciples to take part in a final tea ceremony. The scroll on the tearoom wall was a poem on the evanescence of all things. Rikyu used a particularly fine set of cups and utensils and, after the ceremony was over, presented them to his guests as his final gifts. Then he composed a final poem, after which he slew himself.

Portrait of Soeki Rikyu

CHAPTER TEN

TAKUAN SOHO AND MARTIAL ZEN

One third of D. T. Suzuki's examination of the impact of Zen on Japanese culture deals with Zen and "kendo"—the "way of the sword." In that book, he relates a story about a tea-man, with no martial training, who was attached to the household of a provincial Daimyo. On a particular occasion, the Daimyo insisted that the tea master accompany him on a visit to the capital city, Edo; and, in order that he fit in with the other members of the entourage, he was instructed to dress like a samurai and to carry the two distinctive swords associated with the warrior class.

The tea master was self-conscious about appearing to be something he was not and generally stayed within the compound where they were lodged. However, one day he decided to take a walk to view the sights of the city. While doing so he was accosted by a *ronin*—a masterless samurai. The *ronin* was a bully who could tell by the way the tea master carried himself that he was not a genuine samurai. He blocked the tea master's path and told him, "I see by your dress that you're from the province of Tosa, which is famous for the skill their samurai have with the sword. I would be honored if you would let me test my talents against yours."

The tea-man replied, "I'm not, as you assume, a samurai at all. I have dressed like this at the command of my Lord. I'm a master of *chanoyu*. I know nothing of sword play."

"Then you have no right to carry that sword. But since you have done so, you'll now have to use it regardless of how much or how little you know."

The tea master realized that honor required him to face the *ronin*, and he resigned himself to die in the encounter. However, he did not wish to make a complete fool of himself in the match, which would bring disgrace not only upon himself but upon his Daimyo as well. So he told the *ronin*, "Very well, I will fight you. But at the moment, I am carrying out an errand on behalf of my master. Please allow me to complete it, and I will meet you at this time tomorrow to fulfill my obligation."

The *ronin* agreed to the conditions, and the tea master went in search of someone who could give him rudimentary instruction in *kendo*. He found a training center nearby and knocked at the gate asking to speak with the principal teacher. When he was shown into the sword master's rooms, he described the situation he was in and explained, "I know I can't prevail against an experienced swordsman, but I don't wish to bring disgrace upon my master. I'm here to ask only if you can show me how to die as befits a samurai."

The sword master was surprised by the request and remarked, "Students who come here come to learn how to handle a sword; no one has ever come before me with a request like yours. I'd be honored to show you how to die, as you request, but perhaps you could repay me first by serving me a cup of tea."

The tea master, believing this might be his last opportunity to practice his craft, happily agreed. The implements for the tea ceremony were available at the kendo studio, and the swordsman and the tea-man retired to a small room. The tea master laid aside his borrowed swords and took off his outer robe. Then, giving no thought to the situation in which he found himself, he applied himself to the art of tea. The swordsman observed the single-pointed attention the tea master paid to each step of the process; it was obvious that all superfluous thoughts, including those of the upcoming fight, had been banished and the ritual alone occupied the tea-man's mind.

When the tea master presented the cup to the swordsman, the swordsman congratulated him, "Wonderful! There's nothing you need to learn from me. You already know it all. Maintain the same state of mind you were in while preparing this tea, and that alone will be enough. Treat this *ronin* as if he were a guest coming to your teahouse; welcome him and apologize for having delayed your match. Then, just as you did before preparing the tea, take off your outer robe, bind your brow with the *tenugui* (head scarf), and tie up the sleeves of your robe. Then draw your sword and hold it high over your head with both hands—like this," he said, demonstrating. "Banish all thoughts and wait for him to make the first move. When you hear him give his attack yell, bring your sword down with all your might. If you're fortunate, you may do him a serious injury before he slays you."

The tea-man expressed his gratitude to the swordsman and, the next day, appeared at the appointed place to meet the *ronin*. Following the advice of the sword master, he greeted the *ronin* as he would one who had come to his teahouse. He apologized for having made him wait. Then, with the same mindfulness he brought to *chanoyu*, he took off his robe, tied up his sleeves, and donned the *tenugui*. He took a stable stance, drew his sword, and held it above his head as the master had shown him.

The *ronin* stared in wonder. The tea master who had seemed an easy prey just the day before now appeared to be a formidable opponent. The *ronin* laid his sword on the ground and got on his knees; he bowed to the tea master and begged his forgiveness. Then he rose to his feet and ran off.

The qualities, grounded in Zen discipline, which contributed to making a master of calligraphy or a master tea-man were also applicable to the martial arts, and the Zen master who explored that relationship most thoroughly was Takuan Soho.

Although he left no lineage to succeed him, Takuan was exemplary of the wide scope of Zen influence at the beginning of the Edo period. In addition to being a transmitted Zen teacher, he was also skilled in poetry, *chanoyu*, calligraphy, and painting. He is even credited with having invented the recipe for the popular pickled daikon radish that is called a "Takuan." On top of all that, he was a respected scholar and a prolific author. He sought to resolve the growing rift between neo-Confucionist thought and

Buddhism; he wrote a commentary on the *Xinxin Ming* by the Third Chinese Patriarch (cf. *Zen Masters of China*, Chapter Two); and he wrote about the relationship between Zen and kendo.

He was born in the town of Izushi in 1573, the last year of the Ashikaga Shogunate. His family members were farmers and members of the Pure Land Sect. As a young child, Takuan was enrolled in a Pure Land School, and he practiced the *nembutsu* devoutly— a practice he continued to defend as an older man and Zen abbot.

As a result of his academic prowess, he was sent to Sokoyoji, a Zen temple in the Gozan System, and from there to the Rinka temple, Daitokuji, in Kyoto. There he practiced zazen under the direction of Shunoku Soyen. *Chanoyu* was also taught at Daitokuji and Takuan was introduced to the art of tea. Master Monsai Tonin of Daianji instructed him in Confucian theory, poetry, and calligraphy.

Although a prodigy in many fields, the young Takuan came from a poor family and had little money. He owned only a single robe, and, on one occasion when he hung it out after washing, other students mocked him for having to hide in his room until it was dry. They called him "the naked monk." He responded by suggesting their concern about material possessions hampered their Zen practice. On the other hand, Takuan earned the respect of his teachers, and Master Tonin bequeathed him his substantial library.

Takuan left Daitokuji to continue his zazen practice under Itto Shoteki, the abbot of Yoshunji at Sakai, and it was under Shoteki's guidance that Takuan achieved awakening in 1604. Takuan was identified as Shoteki's heir, and, after the master's death, was appointed abbot of a small, rural temple, Nansoji, in the Daitokuji temple system.

His reputation had begun to grow, and the Emperor Go-Yozei summoned him to Kyoto to be abbot of Daitokuji. It was not a placement with which Takuan was comfortable. Throughout his life, he would be drawn to simplicity and solitude. He preferred small rural temples to the large, competitive training centers in larger cities. He stayed at Daitokuji only three days, then resigned to return to the more congenial environment of Nansoji. However, the turmoil of the larger world would follow him there.

Early in Takuan's life, the perpetual strife between warring clans in Japan had come to an end briefly through the efforts of the Toyotomi clan. Led by Toyotomi Hideyoshi (who had ordered Soeki Rikyu to commit *seppuku*), the clans were briefly unified. Hideyoshi intended his son, Hideyori, to succeed him, but the boy was only five years old when his father died. A council of regents (*tairo*), made up of the five strongest daimyo, was established to rule Japan until the child came of age. It had been Hideyoshi's hope that the five *tairo* would balance one another so that no one of them would become strong enough to seize control of the country. But Tokugawa Ieyasu saw this as an opportunity to claim the shogunate. He established his supremacy at the Battle of Sekigahara, after which the only clan to continue resisting him was the Toyotomi.

Hideyori, only twenty years old, took refuge in the Castle at Osaka. The Tokugawa established their capital at Edo (later renamed Tokyo). Thus began the Edo period, which would provide Japan with 250 years of stable rule. However, before he could feel secure, Ieyasu needed to conquer the last bastion of resistance. In 1614, he laid siege to Osaka Castle, and, the following June, the Toyotomi stronghold was destroyed. The family was decimated. Hideyori committed ritual suicide; his eight-year-old son was captured and taken to Kyoto where he was beheaded.

In the strife leading up to the attack on Osaka Castle, many villages or compounds in outlying areas were destroyed, and, as during the Onin Wars, temples were also targeted. Sugyoji in Takuan's home village was destroyed, as well as Nansoji. Takuan spent the years following the siege of Osaka Castle supervising the rebuilding of both these temples.

After this, weary of the political machinations rife in official Zen circles, he renounced all official status in the hierarchy and took up the life of a wanderer. He traveled the rural areas he loved, visiting small country temples and writing poetry. Eventually, he returned to Sogyoji, where he built a small hermitage. There he dedicated himself to academic study and poetry. When asked if he did not find his isolation burdensome, he replied:

> I feel no loneliness. When my visitors return home, I think to myself, How quiet, how fascinating! And when the sun sets, my questioners leave me to myself. . . . But I remain in this place not to enjoy peace and quiet but because here I have found a resting place for my mind. (38)

In 1627, Takuan became caught up in a dispute between the Shogunate and the Imperial Court over which had authority to appoint the abbots of the Daitoku and Myoshin temples. The Edo government insisted that only individuals who had practiced for at least thirty years and had mastered the 1700 officially sanctioned koans could be appointed abbot. The criteria used by Emperor Go-Mizunoo in making his choices had been less stringent. In a public document, Takuan and two other respected Zen masters argued that the tougher guidelines were unreasonably severe.

The issue was an important one to the Edo government, which was intent on diminishing the relationship between the monasteries and the imperial court. Control of monastic appointments was a significant issue. The shogun declared that Takuan's interference was an act of disloyalty and ordered him banished to Yamagata Prefecture. On the day the edict of exile was carried out, Go-Mizunoo abdicated the throne, leaving it to his daughter, who became the Empress Meisho.

Although he missed Sugyoji, Takuan was made welcome in Yamagata, and there he built another hermitage. After the death of Shogun Hidetada, a general amnesty was declared and Takuan's period of enforced exile came to an end.

In spite of his fondness for solitude and his reclusive lifestyle, Takuan had many friendships with influential people of the day. These included Hidetada's successor, Tokugawa Iemitsu, as well as a number of daimyo, including the Christian, Kuroda Nagamasa; but probably his closest relationship was with a kendomaster in Iemitsu's court, Yagyu Munenori. Takuan's letter to Munenori on "Prajna Immoveable" and its relation to swordsmanship is one of his best known works and a seminal work on the application of Zen principles to other disciplines.

Munenori was the person who invited Takuan to come to Edo after his period of exile, and the two shared a villa until Iemitsu had a small temple for his family, Tokaiji, built outside of the city and named Takuan its founding abbot. Here Takuan spent his final years.

Although he accepted students, and despite requests from both the Shogun and the Emperor that he do so, Takuan chose not to name a successor. As a result no teaching line proceeds from him. His literary legacy, on the other hand, is substantial.

Takuan's letter to Munenori on the "Mystery of Prajna Immove-able" begins by drawing attention to the tendency of the mind to "stop" or "abide" with things rather than flow naturally from one object to another. This is characteristic of *avidya*, or the ignorance that is the opposite of enlightenment. In kendo, if the swords-man's attention is stopped in this manner, he will be unable to respond to the moves of his opponent.

> No doubt you see the sword about to strike you, but do not let your mind "stop" there. Have no intention to coun-terattack him in response to his threatening move, cherish no calculating thoughts whatsoever. You simply perceive the opponent's move, you do not allow your mind to "stop" with it, you move on just as you are toward the opponent and make use of his attack by turning it on to himself. Then his sword meant to kill you will become your own and the weapon will fall on the opponent himself. (39)

This is the sword of "no-sword," in the sense that one is not consciously aware of self or sword but responds spontaneously and naturally to the situation in which one finds oneself. In this state of mind, Takuan writes, even if one were facing ten oppo-nents at once, as long as one's mind does not "stop" with any one of them, one will emerge victorious.

In contrast to the "stopping" mind, or mind of delusion, is Pra-jna [Wisdom] Immoveable. The mind of delusion is the ego-con-sciousness; but behind it, underlying it, is the unmoved Prajna that is the source of one's ego-consciousness, the Self before thoughts arise. While this Prajna/Wisdom is itself "unmoving" (because it does not "stop" with things), it is the source of spontane-ous movement. Prajna Immoveable is the destroyer of illusion.

Takuan uses the example of the popular images of the goddess Kwannon, the Bodhisattva of Compassion, who is traditionally portrayed with multiple arms. Takuan is careful to note that such statues are symbolic and not necessarily representative of an actual being. If the goddess' attention were focused (stopped) on one particular arm, she would be unable to use the others, but if her mind is not stopped, she can use them all naturally. Kwannon is, thus, the exemplar of the awakened individual capable of using all of his or her faculties to their full capacity.

Takuan goes on to note how new kendo students, before they have received any training at all, are often more effective than students who have begun to learn proper technique. The untrained student responds to attacks spontaneously, instinctively moving to ward off blows. Once the student begins to train, he is taught how to stand, how to hold the sword, and is taught a variety of strikes. As the student acquires more and more knowledge, he inevitably starts to think about what should be the appropriate response to a situation. This thinking is an example of "stopping." But as the student continues to train, he eventually comes to a point where he has absorbed the training so thoroughly that he no longer needs to think about his actions. At this point, he approaches the state of mind he had had before beginning his training, when he knew nothing. He has attained no-mind-ness, or *mushin*—"body and limbs perform by themselves what is assigned to them to do with no interference from the mind." (40)

It is the purpose of spiritual training, Takuan points out, to overcome ignorance and attain no-mind-ness, and, as he demonstrates in his letter to Munenori, that training has practical application for the swordsman as for the other Zen-inspired arts.

When he sensed he was nearing the end of his life, Takuan gave instructions to his students that they were not to carry out any particular ceremonies at his funeral; no sacrifices or mourning gifts were to be offered. He did not want a pagoda or other monument built to his memory. On his deathbed, instead of writing a final poem, he took up his brush and wrote the single character for "dream." He was 71 years old.

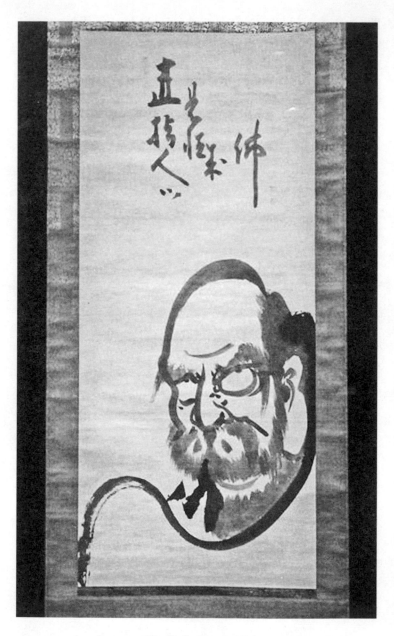

Portrait of Bodhidharma by Hakuin Ekaku

CHAPTER ELEVEN

SUZUKI SHOSAN

Takuan's contemporary, Suzuki Shosan, is an exceptional figure in the history of Japanese Zen. Self-trained and not officially associated with any of the formal Zen schools, he developed a unique practice which, for a short time, was attractive especially to lay people disenchanted with the monastic forms of Zen.

He was the first of seven children born to a family of samurai retainers of the Matsudaira Clan. It was a warrior family, and an unlikely one to produce a major religious figure, although Shosan's mother was said to have had a vision of a Bodhisattva before the birth of her firstborn.

When Shosan was four years old, a cousin of the same age died suddenly, and he asked his parents where his playmate had gone. After the concept of death was explained to him, he became preoccupied with it. It would be the dominant concern of his life. As a young man he strove to overcome his fear of dying by carrying out feats of bravery; he fantasized about fighting sea serpents and exploring the supposedly haunted caves at the foot of Mount Fuji.

He grew to be an able soldier and along with both his father and his brother, Shigenari, fought in the Battle of Sekigahara as well as at the siege of the Castle of Osaka, where he distinguished himself.

Like Takuan's family, Shosan's were members of the Pure Land Sect, and he practiced the *nembutsu* throughout his life. However, like many samurai, he was also familiar with Zen. During his time in service to Tokugawa Ieyasu, Shosan had an opportunity to travel about the country. While doing so, he visited Zen teachers wherever possible. Perhaps because his military responsibilities did not give him the time to do so, he did not work directly under the guidance of any of these teachers; instead, he developed his own practice combining what he learned about zazen with his family's use of the *nembutsu*.

One day while on guard duty at Osaka Castle, Shosan's thoughts turned to the Nio (or Kongorikishi) statues that stand guard at the entrance to some Buddhist temples. These two figures are traditionally shown with scowling expressions and carrying weapons.

It occurred to Shosan that being guardians was their way of serving the Dharma. He determined that, as a soldier, he should serve the Dharma with the same fierce dedication thc Nio brought to their duties.

After the battle for Osaka Castle, the Tokugawa Shogunate was firmly established, and a form of peace settled on the land. Now that there was no longer the same demand for samurai warriors there had been, Shosan requested to be relieved of his obligations as a retainer and be allowed to become a monk; he did so realizing that if his request were denied he might be expected to commit *seppuku*. Ieyasu's heir, Hidetada, gave his permission, and, at the age of 42, the Rinzai master, Daigu Sochiku, ordained Shosan. Because of Shosan's age, Daigu broke with tradition and did not assign him a Buddhist name to supplant his birth name.

Shosan did not remain with Daigu after ordination. Instead he traveled about Japan visiting a number of respected contemporary teachers. He spent some time as a member of the Vinaya School whose teachings focused on the precepts of Buddhist morality. These included the prohibition against eating meat. Shosan had been used to a more substantial diet during his time as a soldier, but he accepted the new restrictions and limited himself to eating barley and rice. Eventually, however, he fell ill, and one of his brothers, a physician, attributed his condition to poor nutrition. From then on, Shosan adhered to a healthier diet that included occasional meat dishes, and he determined that the Vinaya path was not appropriate for men with a military background.

He retained friendly relationships with several Zen masters, including Daigu, Shido Munan, and Gudo Toshoku [Chapter Thirteen], but he did not become a disciple of any of them. Nor did he take up residence in a monastic community, preferring, as had Takuan, to live in private hermitages. Although he had been ordained in the Rinzai tradition, he acquired a poor impression of Rinzai Zen during his travels. The temples he visited often seemed to be centers of art and wealth, and the monks appeared less interested in the religious life than they were in finding a way to live comfortably, free from the demands and travails of secular life.

Serious teachers like Shido Munan recognized that discipline in many monasteries had grown slack, and Munan asked Shosan to write a book outlining a more strenuous practice. The volume Shosan produced was entitled *Fumoto no Kusawake* (*Parting the Grasses at the Foot of the Mountain*). As a result of it, the former samurai gained some fame as a teacher despite the fact that, by his own admission, he still had not had kensho. Students sought out his hermitage in the Ishinotaira Valley, and soon it became a teaching center, although it remained unaffiliated with any of the official Zen schools. There Shosan taught a practice he called Nio Zen.

At the age of 61, he finally had a kensho that left him in a state of ecstasy for thirty days. Later, he would look back upon that experience indifferently:

> —I felt completely detached from life and death and in touch with my true nature. I danced with gratitude, feeling that nothing existed. At that time, you could have threatened me to cut off my head and it wouldn't have meant a thing. Yet after thirty days like this, I decided it didn't suit me. It was nothing more than a realization based on a particular state of mind. So I discarded it and returned to my previous state. I filled my heart with death and practiced uncompromisingly. (41)

Shosan never bothered to have his awakening formally acknowledged, and he would always claim to be "self-enlightened without the aid of a teacher." The experience even led him to question the value of kensho. He was contemptuous of what he called *kitai-zen*, Zen practice undertaken in expectation of attaining some end, such as satori. The Rinzai emphasis on kensho, he argued, resulted in monks with very minor awakening experiences coming to believe they were fully enlightened individuals. Particularly significant to him was the fact that he seldom saw a notable change in the moral behavior of these monks. Their lifestyles, preoccupied as they were with physical comfort and ambitions to advance within the hierarchy, were evidence of how preoccupied they remained with Self or Ego.

He did not deny the reality of the kensho experience, but he made use of the ten Ox-Herding pictures (42) to stress that there were degrees of awareness. Even in his eighties, he told students that he had not yet come to full awakening and was blunt in contesting the Rinzai assertion that satori was essential to Zen. "Those who believe that there is no value in Buddhism without satori are mistaken. The goal of Buddhism is to make proper use of your mind in this very moment." Buddhism, for Shosan, was not the attainment of a particular experience or way of perception; rather, it was a way of living one's life.

His views were closer to those of the Soto tradition than they were to the Rinzai, and while he was never officially associated with it, Shosan respected the Soto School. Soto Zen was the form most popular with the lower classes. Rinzai practitioners referred to it as "farmer Zen," which, in Shosan's opinion, was one of the things that made the tradition attractive. Where the emphasis in Rinzai was on awakening and demonstrating the depth of one's understanding by passing an elaborate and formalized system of koans, Soto stressed that practice consisted not only of seated meditation but also in carrying out one's daily labors in a mindful way.

Shosan wanted to establish a form of Zen available to everyone, not just an elite few sequestered in monastic communities. He found what he wanted in the practice of mindfulness and an acceptance of one's station in life. He was a social conservative who believed that the circumstances of one's birth were determined not by chance but were the result of karmic influences carried over from previous lives. Therefore the correct way to work out one's present destiny was by fulfilling the duties associated with the class into which one had been born. A samurai should practice samurai Zen; a farmer, farmer Zen.

Shosan claimed that the samurai, because their training taught them to hold their own lives lightly, were particularly suited to this practice. A samurai must be able to maintain his practice even in the midst of battle; for such a one, the quiet, passive zazen of monastics was of no value whatsoever. So although he himself had left military life to become a monk, he discouraged others from following his example.

The particular spiritual practice an individual undertook was less important than the manner in which they pursued it. Whether they practiced zazen, recited the *nembutsu*, or chanted sutras, the important point was that they do so with the martial spirit of the Nio. Shosan instructed people to keep the Chinese character for Death in their heart and to use it as a goad to give their practice energy. People should follow the example of the Nio even to the extent of assuming a fierce expression and "glaring like Bodhidharma." He told them to activate their *ki*, that vital energy which the samurai cultivated and called upon during the heat of battle. The Buddha-way, Shosan insisted, was not an easy path. It required strenuous effort and continuous practice persisted in over more than one lifetime.

At times he appears to be contemptuous of human life. He referred to his own body, for example, variously as a "bag of excrement," a "bag of worms," and even an "idiotic bag of pains and sorrows." What he was emphasizing was the importance of not being attached to either the physical or mental Self. As a result, his was a very austere and demanding form of Zen, and yet it was also a Zen that could be practiced by lay people of all classes.

The same themes occur over and over in the stories told about Shosan—a reminder to keep mindful of death and to carry out the responsibilities appropriate to one's station in life.

For example, when a monk asked Shosan to assign him a koan, Shosan told him to keep his attention focused on the character for Death—no other koan, he said, was necessary. "Keep that alone in your heart and let all else go."

Another was told, "Repeat to yourself, endlessly, 'I am going to die! I am going to die!'"

A samurai approached Shosan saying that he was considering becoming a monk. Shosan discouraged him from doing so, telling him, "In fact, a samurai is more suited to religious practice than a monk is."

"Why, then, did you abandon your duty to serve Lord Hidetada and become a monk?"

"It was my karma. As a result of actions in previous lives I was drawn to become a monk. For you, it is more appropriate to remain a samurai."

Shosan attended the funeral of a young man who had died quite unexpectedly. He observed the mourners talking amongst themselves and expressing surprise that death had come so early for the deceased.

"What fools they are," Shosan told his disciples. "It is always the same, however. People believe that it is only others who die. They ignore the fact that it is their fate as well. So they pursue trivial things and live their lives as if immune to death. They plan and scheme and are surprised and unprepared when death comes upon them unexpectedly."

An old woman came to Shosan and told him she knew very little about Buddhism. She asked if he could tell her what its major teachings were.

"All you need to know," Shosan told her, "is that you will die! You will die! Imagine! Not one person who lived a hundred years ago is alive today. Not a trace of them remains. Recite *Namu Amida Butsu* and never forget Death."

A man who made his living hunting birds came to Shosan. "My occupation is one that requires me to break the precept against taking life, but what choice do I have? It is what I must do in order to feed my family. Is there anything I can do to achieve salvation and avoid hell?"

"What is important is that you kill the mind—kill the self. Every time you shoot a bird, seize hold of your own mind and kill it as well. If you can kill the self, you will attain Buddhahood even as a hunter."

While Shosan was visiting a temple in Saitama, a group of farmers attended one of his public talks. Afterwards, they asked how they could best practice the Buddha way.

"There is no better way than by farming," Shosan told them. "You have the responsibility for feeding the people; this is an expression of the Buddhist activity of compassion. If you keep your mind focused on your actions, then your body is the Buddha body, your mind is the Buddha mind, and your work Buddha work. Cultivate the land and recite the *nembutsu*. Nothing more is required."

There was a monk whose name, Jihon, meant "fundamental self." For a while he studied with Shosan; then he decided to go out into the world. Shosan's final directions to him included a play on his name:

> Never teach of salvation in a future world of which you are not [yet] a part. Just rouse the truth within yourself and show it to others. As a rule, you will have trouble even in this life when you pretend to be what you are not. Just recite the *nembutsu* so completely that you are released from your self. By being released from your self, I mean that while reciting *Namu Amida Butsu Namu Amida Butsu*, you study death. Death opens up and is clarified. You, too, are treasuring your fundamental self. It doesn't require a lot of time. With the *nembutsu* alone, you can exhaust this self completely. (43)

One day a Rinzai monk challenged Shosan about his practice of the *nembutsu*. "All day long you recite this, but is it really of any value?"

"When I chant *Namu Amida Butsu*," Shosan explained, "what I am really saying is, 'Do away with all attachments!' Surely that is a valuable lesson to keep in mind. I only chant *Namu Amida Butsu* instead because it is easier to say."

A monk complained: "When I am seated in zazen and my thoughts become still, I often become sleepy and struggle to stay awake. What should I do?"

"Rouse yourself, get to your feet, and do dancing zazen," Shosan told him.

Shosan was a vigorous opponent of both Christianity and Confucianism, and he campaigned to have Buddhism declared the national religion of Japan. He was unsuccessful because many members of the upper classes were drawn to the neo-Confucionist movement, viewing Buddhism as an impractical and otherworldly tradition. They believed that, in contrast, Confucianism was practical and that its tenets contributed to establishing a well-ordered society. Shosan wrote a tract contesting that point of view.

He wrote an even more vigorous attack on Christianity, *Ha Kirishitan*. Christian missionaries had been active in Japan since the middle of the 16th century. Both civic and religious leaders considered the western religion a disruptive social influence. It certainly differed from the other religious traditions in Japan that were able to make accommodations with one another. Christianity, on the other hand, professed that its teachings alone were the truth and condemned all other belief systems—including Buddhism and Shinto—not only as false doctrines but as evil ones.

When it became obvious that the intention of the missionaries was to attempt to convert all of Japan, tensions arose. Certain pragmatic noble families had converted to Christianity as a way of furthering commerce with Portuguese merchants who provided them with—among other things—arms. One of these families was the Arima of Shimabara. Following the example of their lords, much of the populace of Shimabara also accepted Christianity.

While Ieyasu had been tolerant of Christians, Hidetada was not. He limited foreign merchants to the port of Nagasaki and actively proscribed missionary activity. Hidetada's successor, Iemitsu, was even more aggressive in seeking to quell Christian expansionism. He had fifty converts burned alive as part of the ceremonies marking his ascension to the Shogunate. Iemitsu pursued an isolationist policy. Foreigners were expelled from the country; an artificial island was constructed in Nagasaki Harbor where the few remaining merchants were kept in seclusion. All Japanese citizens were compelled to register as members of Buddhist Temples. Christian families were dispossessed. Matsukura Shigemasa who immediately began construction of a new castle of notable extravagance and expense replaced the Arima in Shimabara. The costs were covered by taxation. The peasants of Shimabara rose up in rebellion and occupied the abandoned Hara Castle from which they flew flags adorned with the sign of the cross. Although the Shimabara Rebellion of 1637-38 is sometimes described as a Christian uprising, it was actually a tax revolt.

The Dutch, seeking to regain some of their former influence in the country—and with no regard for the welfare of their coreligionists—supplied the Shogunate with ships and cannons that were used to bombard Hara Castle. The stronghold was destroyed and all the occupants executed.

After the rebellion was put down, Shosan's brother, Shigenari, was assigned to a political post in the region. Shosan joined him there in 1642, and the two brothers founded a total of thirty-two temples—thirty-one Soto temples and one Pure Land temple—to promote and preserve Buddhism in the region.

Shigenari came to have sympathy with the plight of the people in the district; he recognized that the taxes demanded of them were beyond their abilities to meet, and, in 1653, he requested the authorities to show greater leniency in the matter. His request was denied, and Shigenari committed *seppuku*.

After his brother's death, Shosan spent his final years in Edo where he lived in a small two-mat room. Two years later, he fell ill, and the doctor who was called in to examine him reported that his case was terminal. Undisturbed by the prognosis, Shosan commented, "I dealt with my own death more than thirty years ago."

Portrait of Ingen Ryuki

CHAPTER TWELVE

FOUR 17TH CENTURY MASTERS

GUDO TOSHOKU

SHIDO MUNAN

INGEN RYUKI

DOKUTAN SHOKEI

GUDO TOSHOKU

Myoshinji, the modest temple originally built by Kanzan, evolved over time into a Kyoto complex and became the largest school in the Rinzai tradition. At the beginning of the Edo Period, its most significant abbot was Gudo Toshoku. He entered religious life at the age of eight and, as a young man, traveled about Japan visiting several Rinzai temples. He attained awakening in 1628 and his understanding of Zen was so well respected that he became the private teacher of the retired emperor, Go-Yozei, as a result of which he was given the posthumous title of Kokushi.

The most famous preserved dialogue between the emperor and the Zen master is probably a combination of several conversations. It begins with Go-Yozei saying, "It is my understanding that according to the teachings of Zen this very mind, just as it is, is Buddha. Is that correct?"

"If I agree with what you say," Gudo responded, "your majesty will believe you understand without actually doing so. However, if I deny what you say, I will be denying something well known to all."

"Then tell me," the retired emperor persisted, "a man who comes to enlightenment—what happens to him after he dies?"

"I don't know," Gudo admitted.

"You don't know? Aren't you an enlightened teacher?"

"I am. But not a dead one," Gudo pointed out.

The emperor was stymied for a moment, unsure how to proceed. Just before he started to speak again, Gudo brought his hand down hard on the wooden floor and the sound brought the emperor to awakening.

With imperial support, Gudo was able to travel throughout the Japanese isles restoring and founding temples. He served three separate terms as abbot of Myoshinji. Towards the end of his life, he settled at a small temple in Kyoto. There he is said to have reflected back on his life's activity and remarked: "After all these years of journeying about, here I am knocking at the gates of Zen. I have to laugh. My staff is broken; my umbrella torn. And the teaching of the Buddha is so simple: when hungry, eat; when thirsty, drink; when cold, wrap yourself in a good warm cloak."

Gudo left few written records behind, but a story is told which demonstrates the respect with which he was held. According to the tale, as an old man he still gave talks to the retired Emperor and members of his court. On one occasion, the elderly Zen master dozed off in the middle of his sermon. Rather than wake him, the emperor signaled everyone to stand quietly and leave, allowing the venerable teacher to rest undisturbed.

Just before he died, Gudo wrote: "My task is done. Now those who follow me must work for the benefit of all humankind." After writing these words, he laid his brush down, yawned, and passed away.

SHIDO MUNAN

One of the temples for which Gudo had responsibility was located at Sekigahara, where the battle had taken place that established the primacy of the Tokugawa Clan. When Gudo was in the region, he stayed at a local inn and there he took an interest in the innkeeper's son. The boy was being trained in the family business but showed intellectual promise above his station. Locally, he was known as the "*Kana*-writing boy" because of his skill in the cursive form of the Japanese syllabic script.

When he was fourteen years old, the boy accompanied his father to the old capital, Kyoto. Along the way, they passed through regions that had been devastated during the recent civil conflicts. These sights left a lasting impression on the boy, and, when he was in Kyoto, he made contact with Master Gudo and took up a lay practice of Zen.

In the Rinzai system, students were first taught *susokkan*, counting the breaths. When they achieved some degree of concentration, they were instructed to focus on the breath without counting. And, finally, when the student was deemed ready, the teacher would assign him a koan. The koan Gudo gave to the innkeeper's son was taken from the poem written by the Chinese Sixth Patriarch, Huineng: "—from the beginning not a thing exists." [cf. *Zen Masters of China*, Chapter Three]

Before he could complete his Zen training, the young man had to return to Sekigahara to take up his duties at the family inn. Whenever Gudo was in the area he would check on the boy's progress. A number of decades passed in this manner. The boy grew to adulthood, married, and became his father's successor as innkeeper. Over time, he fell away from his practice of Zen and acquired a taste for sake and gambling.

Around the year 1656, Gudo was once more in the region and stopped at the inn to see how his former student was doing. When he arrived, he was greeted by the innkeeper's wife who told the

Zen master that her husband was out. She invited him to come in to wait for him, and, as the two sat together, they fell into easy conversation, during the course of which the wife confided that her husband had taken to drinking in recent years.

"When he drinks," she said, "he can become abusive. He also gambles when he has too much to drink, and he always loses. Really, there are times when I think my children and I would be better off without him. But he's my husband—what can I do?"

"Let me see what I can do," Gudo suggested. "It's late. You retire, and I'll wait for your husband. But before you leave, would you please bring me a bottle of your best sake and two cups."

The woman did as Gudo asked. Then she gathered her children together, and they retired to the sleeping quarters. Gudo remained in the main room of the inn, seated in meditation. Around midnight, the innkeeper returned home in a drunken-state and was embarrassed to find his teacher there. Gudo did not reprimand him for his behavior and, in fact, indicated the bottle of sake set out on a table. Gudo invited the innkeeper to share a cup with him, to which the man readily agreed. The two had several cups of wine, chatting idly, and eventually the innkeeper fell asleep on the floor.

When he woke the next morning, he found Gudo still seated in meditation before the family shrine.

"You are awake," Gudo noted. "And it is time for me to return to the capital."

The man was a little hung-over and humiliated that his teacher had seen him in such a disreputable condition. He mumbled a reply.

As Gudo tied his sandals, he remarked, "You know, human life is brief and all things pass away. When you spend your time drinking and gambling, you have no time for other things that may be much more important. Besides which, you bring sorrow to your family and those who depend upon you."

The innkeeper broke into tears and admitted that he had known for some time he needed to change his behavior. He swore an oath to do so, starting that very day, and, as a sign of gratitude, he asked Gudo to allow him to carry his bags on the first stage of his journey. Gudo agreed and the two set off. When they had gone a fair distance, Gudo told the man he should return home. But the man asked to be allowed to accompany the Zen master a little further. Eventually they arrived at the next village, and, once again Gudo offered to take up his own bags. The man said he was willing to accompany Gudo a bit further.

The next time Gudo offered to take up his bags, the man shook his head, "I'll go with you all the way to Edo."

Once they came to the city, the man had his head shaved and entered monastic life at the age of 52. Gudo gave him the name Shido Munan, a phrase found in *Xinxin Ming* of the third Chinese Patriarch, Jianzhi Sengcan. [cf. *Zen Masters of China*, Chapter Two] The first line of the poem, in Japanese, reads "The Perfect Way (*shido*) has no difficulties (*munan*)."

After he achieved awakening, Munan underwent a radical change of life-style. He did not, however, become active in the Rinzai hierarchy. Like his master, Gudo, he recognized that the tradition was stagnating. The career and political aspirations of monks made up a large part of the problem. Even monks who had achieved awakening were subject to ambitions. The koan training system had been compromised; correct "answers" could be purchased from older monks; some monks discovered they had a knack for coming up with appropriate answers without necessarily having insight. In addition, temple schools often drew students more interested in developing skills in literature or the arts than in Zen training.

Traditionally, the emphasis in Rinzai training had been on the attainment of awakening, but Munan recognized that while awakening was important, it was not an end in itself. Rather he saw it as an aid that helped the monk reform his character. Awakening, he asserted, was relatively easy to attain. Practicing the way of the Buddha, on the other hand, was difficult, especially for one who had not seen into his true nature.

> Even though a man leaves his home and lives simply with his three robes and a bowl on a rock under a tree, he still cannot be called a true Buddhist priest. . . . Yet if he does wish earnestly to become a true priest, he will realize that he has many desires and is possessed of a body which is endowed with eighty-four thousand evils, of which the cardinal five are sexual desire, cupidity, birth-and-death, jealousy, and desire for fame. These evils are the way of the world. They are by no means easy to overcome. Day and night, by means of enlightenment [awakening], you should set yourself to eliminating them one after another, thus purifying yourself. (44)

Munan provided an example to others of the change in life he expected Zen practitioners to attain. He was a close friend of and mentor to Suzuki Shosan, who shared his opinions on many topics. Munan lived frugally in a hermitage with few physical comforts and gathered a small group of disciples around him who were able to emulate his ascetic lifestyle. Of these, only one would be designated his heir—Dokyo Etan.

INGEN RYUKI

Munan's asceticism was one response to the spiritual malaise into which the Rinzai School had fallen, as was Suzuki Shosan's secular Nio-Zen. Another response was the Obaku School.

Because of the isolationist policies of the current Shogunate, there were few foreigners in the Japanese isles. Chinese businessmen, however, had been allowed to set up a small community in Nagasaki. There, in circumstances similar to those that would bring Shunryu Suzuki to San Francisco in the 1950s, these merchants sent messages back to China asking that Chinese priests be sent to minister to them. They were not looking for spiritual direction; they wanted Buddhist clerics who would offer rites with which they were familiar, rituals to petition the gods to protect their ships and cargo, rituals to mark the transitions points in life—births, marriages, funerals, and anniversary rites.

The first group of Chinese missionaries, which arrived in 1620, included Dosha Chogen (Daozhe Chaoyuan), who would become one of Bankei Yotaku's teachers. Dosha was a strong teacher and gathered a number of disciples, but Dosha was eclipsed by a second Chinese teacher, Ingen Ryuki (Yinyuan Longqi), who came to Nagasaki at the invitation of the local authorities. Ingen was already a well-known teacher in China, and a rivalry broke out between his followers and those of Dosha, which eventually resulted in Dosha returning to China.

Ingen was fleeing the turmoil then occurring in China after the collapse of the Ming Dynasty, and he welcomed the opportunity to travel to Japan. He brought with him some twenty disciples and a group of artisans skilled in the architectural techniques then current in China.

Ingen's fame preceded him, and he received a warm welcome in Nagasaki. As a foreigner, there were restrictions placed on his movements, but he managed to find friends who intervened on his behalf. He soon acquired a large number of Japanese disciples.

Because Ingen could trace his Dharma lineage directly back to the founder of the Rinzai School, Rinzai Gigen (Linji Yixuan, cf. *Zen Masters of China*, Chapter Fifteen), some of these Japanese followers hoped that Ingen would be appointed abbot of Myoshinji.

Other members of the Rinzai community, including Gudo Toshoku, were not comfortable with the suggested appointment. They objected to what they considered the "foreign flavor" of Ingen's Zen. Although the Japanese Rinzai School had been based on Tang and Song Dynasty models, those traditions had been modified over time and were now thoroughly assimilated into Japanese culture. The Ming Dynasty Zen of Ingen and his followers seemed peculiar. The chants were unfamiliar and set to Chinese melodies which sounded odd to the Japanese ear. The imagery of the Buddhas and Bodhisattvas was unusual. But the most off-putting element was the inclusion of Pure Land practices, in particular the recitation of the *nembutsu*, which many Japanese Rinzai priests still considered out of keeping with their practice, but which Ingen and his followers refused to curtail.

As a result, Ingen's appointment to Myoshinji was successfully blocked. Ingen's first inclination was to return to China, but his followers encouraged him to remain and arranged for a temple to be built for him on the hills of Uji, outside of Kyoto. Ingen called the hill Obaku (Huangbo) after the Chinese site where his former monastery had been located. The temple was named Manpukuji. The artisans who had formed part of Ingen's entourage when he arrived in Japan were able to construct a building in Chinese Ming Style.

Ingen considered Manpukuji a Rinzai temple, but the Rinzai establishment did not. The result was that it inadvertently became the main temple of a third and new Zen school—known as the Obaku School from the temple's location. The temple differed in a number of respects from Japanese temples, not only in physical form but in practices as well. Ingen's monastic rules followed Chinese protocols rather than Japanese. Even the way the monks ate differed. Instead of using the nested *orioki* bowls Japanese monks were provided with, the meals at Manpukuji were served from a single bowl around which monks gathered and into which they dipped their chopsticks communally.

The new sect had some initial success, drawing prospective students away from Rinzai schools like Myoshinji, which only irritated the Japanese hierarchy further. Some of these students may have been drawn to Manpukuji because of its exotic atmosphere, but others were seeking spiritual guidance which they were no longer certain they could find in the Rinzai or Soto traditions.

The new school expanded quickly. By the time of Ingen's death, he had established twenty-four Obaku temples in Japan.

DOKUTAN SHOKEI

The first abbots at Manpukuji all came from China. They brought with them a style of Zen that, like the Nio Zen of Suzuki Shosan, incorporated elements of the Pure Land School. A unique characteristic of the school was the dual practice of chanting the *nembutsu* while holding in the mind the question (koan) "Who is chanting?"

The fourth abbot of Manpukuji was Dokutan Shokei (Duzhan Xingying) who put so much emphasis on the *nembutsu* that some questioned whether he was actually a Zen teacher.

A story is told about a devout *nembutsu* practitioner named Enjo who kept the name of the Amida Buddha in mind constantly both day and night. Eventually through this method he attained awakening and went to Manpukuji to have the abbot, Dokutan, confirm it.

When Dokutan saw him, he asked, "Where do you come from?"

"Yamashiro," Enjo replied.

"What practice do you follow?"

"Pure Land."

"Tell me then, how old is Amida Buddha?"

"The same age as I am."

"How old are you?"

"The same age as Amida Buddha."

"And where is Amida Buddha now?"

Enjo closed his left fist and raised it.

"Ah!" Dokutan said, delighted. "You are indeed a follower of the Pure Land!"

After the collapse of the Gozan System, reforms within the Rinzai School would curb the appeal of the Obaku School. However, it still remains active in Japan, although it is relatively small compared to the Soto and Rinzai traditions.

Landscape by Sesshu Toyo

CHAPTER THIRTEEN

BANKEI YOTAKU

Bankei was born into a Confucian family in the year 1622. His father died when the boy was only 10, and Bankei's elder brother, Masaysu, became the head of the family that consisted of five brothers and four sisters along with their mother. Masaysu, like his father, was a practitioner of Chinese medicine and a person of some stature in their community. The younger brother, on the other hand, did not at first show much promise. He was headstrong and undisciplined. Masaysu had to instruct the ferryman who transported the boy across the river to his school not to let Bankei return from classes early. Bankei responded by wading the river on foot, holding his breath as he went under until he came back into the shallows.

The standard method of instruction at Confucian schools consisted in the memorization and recitation of major Confucian texts. It was dull work to which students applied themselves listlessly, seldom paying much attention to the meaning of the passages they committed to memory; however, when Bankei was ten years old he was struck by a passage from the *Daigaku* [*The Great Learning*] which stated that "the Great Wisdom illuminates bright virtue." The boy asked his teacher what Confucius meant by "bright virtue." The teacher, quoting a traditional gloss on the passage, replied that it referred to the "inherent nature of goodness in persons."

"What is that inherent nature?" Bankei persisted.

"It is your basic nature."

"But what does that mean? What does it refer to? How can I come to know my basic nature?"

The teacher admitted that he did not have the answer to that question. The question stayed with Bankei and became, for him, that "great doubt" which can lead one to the quest for awakening.

The boy took to speaking with the itinerant monks who passed through his village, asking them if they could clarify the matter of bright virtue and one's basic nature. The monks told him that if he were sincere, he should find a teacher who could guide him in the Buddha Dharma. Bankei spent so much time in this quest that he neglected his schoolwork. Eventually, Masaysu felt compelled to take the extreme measure of casting Bankei out of the household, even though he was only eleven years old.

A family friend provided the boy with a small hut, which Bankei gave the grandiose name of *Shugyoan* (Hermitage of Practice). He wrote the name on a plank he set up outside its door. In this small hut, he dedicated himself to the spiritual practices he had been able to glean from local sources. At a local Pure Land temple, he was introduced to the *nembutsu*, and he applied himself to that for a while. Then he spent a period of time at a nearby Shingon Temple. But neither of these was able to help him discover what either basic nature or luminous virtue was.

At 16, Bankei sought out the Zen master Umpo Zenjo at Zuioji in Ako. Umpo told him that the only way to discover basic nature was through the practice of zazen. Bankei sensed that perhaps here was a teacher who could help him, and he became a monk, receiving the Buddhist name Yotaku. For three years, he remained at Zuioji, but came no closer to finding an answer to his questions. Although he retained respect for Umpo, Bankei decided he needed to pursue his quest elsewhere.

He left Zuioji and traveled from monastery to monastery seeking someone who could resolve his persistent doubt. Frequently he had nowhere to stay and slept out in the open or stayed with beggars, including, for a time, with the beggars under the Gojo Bridge in Kyoto where the Emperor Hanazono had found Shuho Myocho. Throughout all of this, he continued the practice of zazen he had learned from Umpo.

He went on in this manner for four years; then, nearly in despair, he returned to Zuioji, where he told Umpo that he had not been able to find a teacher who could resolve his doubt.

"Your difficulty is that you persist in looking for someone else to help you," Umpo told him bluntly. "That's what prevents you from attaining your goal."

Understanding from Umpo that he could only find what he sought within himself, Bankei moved into a straw hut not far from Zuioji. It was four and a half mats large, and Bankei compared it to a prison cell. He sealed off the door, leaving only a small opening for monks from Zuioji to pass him food. There he applied himself so intensively to zazen that sores broke out on his buttocks and legs from the extended sitting. He fought sleep by dousing himself with cold water and drove himself with all of his energy.

The effort was too much for his health, and he contracted a pulmonary disease that may have been tuberculosis. He coughed up blood and was so sick that the monks from Zuioji brought a physician to see him. The physician declared that the disease had progressed too far to be treated. Bankei was resigned to the situation. Huddled in his small hut, unable to take any nourishment save for a little broth, he waited for death. His throat filled with phlegm as he sat there in misery, and he spat it out. A gob struck the wall and slid down. As he watched it, Bankei suddenly experienced *kensho*. All things, he later declared, were perfectly resolved in what he called "the Unborn."

Slowly his health improved. Both his appetite and strength returned. He opened the door of the hermitage, allowing in clean air. One day, as he continued his zazen, he caught the scent of the flowering plum trees. This occasioned an even deeper awakening, and he found within himself the answers to his questions about basic nature and luminous virtue.

When he was strong enough to do so, he went to see Umpo and reported his experiences. "You now have the marrow of Bodhidharma," Umpo told him, "but I'm not sure how deep your understanding goes." He suggested that the younger man travel to Daisenji in order to ask the famous Gudo Toshoku to verify his enlightenment.

When Bankei arrived at Daisenji, Gudo was away on one of the trips he had to make in order to supervise the many temples under his charge. Bankei went to a number of other teachers in the region, but he could tell that none of them had the authority or insight to verify his enlightenment. He found a number of monks willing to talk about Zen, but they admitted frankly that they had not attained awakening themselves. Rather, they based their teachings on the experiences and written records of teachers from the past. Bankei compared their efforts to trying to scratch an itchy foot without taking off one's shoe.

On the one hand Bankei was disappointed at the sorry state to which Zen had fallen in Japan; on the other he became certain that his own insight must be one of the most profound to have occurred in recent years. Umpo was less confident of his pupil's attainment and suggested that if Gudo were unavailable Bankei should go to Nagasaki and meet the Chinese Zen master, Dosha Chogen, who was then teaching at Sofukuji.

Bankei's meetings with Dosha were complicated by the fact that neither spoke the other's language; however, they could both read Chinese characters. By exchanging written messages, Bankei described his experiences to Dosha. The Zen master replied, writing: "You have understood the matter of self, but to master the depths of our school you must go even deeper."

Bankei was aware of how much more profound his insight was than that of the other teachers he had met. He had been confident that he was already fully awakened and had only wanted Dosha to confirm the fact. Surprised and affronted by Dosha's remark, Bankei stood and left the room without the courtesy of bowing.

However, something about the Zen master's manner and comportment nagged at Bankei, and he did not leave Sofukuji. He eventually humbled himself and asked Dosha to accept him as a pupil. He joined the community of Dosha's disciples and worked in the kitchen and served meals to the other monks. However, he resisted taking part in the Chinese rituals and forms Dosha made use of, arguing that he was focused on awakening and had no time to waste on learning foreign procedures. This included refusing to take part in koan training, which Dosha formally conducted in

Chinese. Throughout his career, Bankei would express skepticism about the value of koan study.

He had his third and most profound enlightenment experience at Sofukuji, where he immediately presented himself to Dosha. He wrote: "What is the great issue of Buddhism?"

Dosha took the brush and replied: "Whose issue?"

Bankei thrust out his arms. Dosha started to write again, but, before the brush touched the paper, Bankei grabbed it. Then he turned on his heel and strode from the room.

After this interview, Dosha acknowledged Bankei's full enlightenment and sought to appoint him senior monk at Sokufuji. Bankei declined the honor, but other monks were aware it had been made. Many of them already felt that Bankei had been shown special privileges by being excused from partaking in the Chinese rituals; their animosity grew when they learned that he had been offered the position of senior monk. When the situation grew worse, Dosha advised Bankei to leave the monastery.

Bankei went to the mountains of Yoshino, a favorite haunt of Buddhist hermits, and there he attracted his first disciples. Then, in 1654, he returned to Nagasaki and found Dosha's followers in contention with those of the newly arrived Ingen Ryuki. Bankei was loyal to his own teacher and dismissive of Ingen's Zen and the Obaku School he established. Generally, however, both secular and religious leaders held Ingen in higher regard. Bankei tried to assist Dosha in finding a way to stay in Japan; he searched for a suitable temple where Dosha could be installed. But the efforts were fruitless, and, in 1658, Dosha returned to China.

Before he left, Dosha was asked if any of his students had come to full enlightenment. He replied, "Only Bankei."

Now recognized as the heir of both Dosha and Umpo, Bankei began a thirty-six year career as a teacher. He was associated with a number of major temples, but he also maintained a smaller hermitage—Oshiken—where he gathered a select group of disciples. In 1672, he was installed as abbot of Myoshinji.

Reflecting back on his own trials, he now considered the strict austerities he had undertaken to be "useless efforts." He told his disciples that such extremes of behavior were unnecessary, and he appears to have believed that he could bring others to awakening with the simple instruction that they keep in their "Unborn-mind." When challenged by a monk who insisted that all the great masters of the past, including Bankei, had undertaken strenuous efforts, Bankei told him to imagine a group of travelers who had lost their way in the mountains without water and were suffering great thirst. One of the members of the group sets off to seek water on his own, breaking through rough terrain and overcoming many hardships before he succeeds in his quest. The water he returns with would refresh those who had stayed behind and there would be no need for them to undergo the same struggles.

> My own struggle was undertaken mistakenly, because I didn't meet up with a clear-eyed master. Eventually, though, I discovered the Buddha-mind for myself; ever since, I have been telling others about theirs, so they'll know about it without going through that ordeal, just as those people drink water and quench their thirst without having to go and find it for themselves. (45)

Throughout his career, in addition to conducting meditation retreats, Bankei frequently gave talks that were open to men and women of all classes. Contrary to the common prejudice of the day, Bankei asserted that women were endowed with the same Unborn Buddha-mind as men. In a sermon given at Hoshinji he even suggested that it was easier for women to attain awakening than it was for men, who were often hampered by intellectual pretensions.

He did not write down his talks, and he expressly forbade his followers to write down what he said—a command they ignored, as a result of which there is a substantial record of his teachings now available. At the core of Bankei's teaching is the concept of the Unborn Buddha-mind with which, he asserted, all persons were endowed. Over and over, he insisted that each receives this Unborn Buddha-mind from his parents, that it is a human birthright. In one comparison, he described it as being like the sun that shines even when obscured by clouds. The Buddha-mind is clear and active in each person even though it may be obscured by the clouds of illusion.

Bankei's teaching and the vocabulary he used were very different from those of other Zen masters, and his detractors cast doubt on whether he was actually awakened, something they could more easily do because he had not bothered to keep the certificate of *inka* presented to him by Dosha. Others questioned whether what he taught was actually Buddhism and even suggested he might be a Christian. These criticisms hampered him early in his teaching career. His charismatic personality, however, made him a convincing speaker, and he soon had Rinzai, Soto, and Obaku monks in his audiences, as well as Tendai, Shingon, and Pure Land practitioners.

He had the ability to present his ideas in an easily graspable manner. To explain what he meant by the Unborn Buddha-mind, for example, he asked people to consider what happened while they were attending one of his talks. They focused their attention carefully on everything he said; however, if they heard a dog bark at the same time as Bankei was speaking they would immediately know what it was and not mistake it for the call of a bird or other animal. The mind that knows this, without any conscious intention to know, is the Unborn Buddha-mind.

> None of you could say that you heard the sounds because you had made up your minds to hear them beforehand. If you did, you wouldn't be telling the truth. All of you are looking this way intent upon hearing me. You're concentrating single-mindedly on listening. There's no thought in any of your minds to hear the sounds or noises that might occur behind you. You are able to hear and distinguish sounds when they do occur without consciously intending to hear them because you're listening by means of the unborn Buddha-mind. (46)

One who is able to live in accord with the Unborn Buddha-mind no longer dwells in illusion, and not to dwell in illusion is precisely to be a Buddha. That, he tells his listeners, is what they desire. The reason they came to his talks is not because they sought to become Buddhists, but rather because they desired to become Buddhas, which was their natural state.

It is preoccupation with the deluded-self, what Bankei calls "self-partiality," which prevents people from being aware of the Unborn Buddha-mind. The ego-self cannot see clearly because its vision is clouded by the poisons of greed, anger, and ignorance from which emotions and personal ambitions arise. The Unborn Buddha-mind, on the other hand, is free from both thought and all forms of self-partiality and is, therefore, able to deal with all situations naturally and perfectly.

When asked what one should do to come into harmony with the Unborn, Bankei explained that since all persons had already received the Unborn mind at birth there was nothing one could do to "attain" it. If one felt called to do zazen or recite sutras or the *nembutsu*, one should do so. Otherwise, all one had to do was attend to one's work with no other thoughts. That, in itself, was the Unborn Buddha-mind at work.

Unlike most teachers, Bankei offered a teaching accessible to everyone. His talks were popular in large part because of the simple and homely examples he used to make his points. "Imagine," he said, "a woman who is sewing while she listens to a friend chatting. As long as she remains in the Unborn Mind, she has no difficulty doing both things at once. But if she were to focus on the conversation, she'd start thinking about what response she should make to her friend, and her hands would stop sewing as she searches for the right thing to say. It's those thoughts which pull her away from the Unborn Mind, and because of which her mind loses its natural freedom."

His lectures were not universally admired. On one occasion a priest from a rival sect interrupted his talk, by shouting: "What is this nonsense you're spouting? I can't understand a word you're saying."

"Oh," Bankei said apologetically, "I am sorry. Please come forward so we can discuss this."

The priest swaggered up to the teaching platform and stood expectantly

"Please come to my side," Bankei urged him.

The priest did so.

"Not that side, please. My hearing isn't so good in that ear."

The priest moved to his other side.

"There," Bankei said. "See how well you understand me after all! Now please be still and listen."

Another rival priest challenged him saying, "The founder of our sect had such powers that if an attendant held up a sheet of paper on one side of the river, he could write the name of the Buddha in the air on the other side of the river, and it would appear on the paper. What do you think of that?"

"Not much. Stage magicians are capable of much more spectacular feats," Bankei scoffed. "But that isn't the way of Zen."

"No? What 'feats' are you capable of?"

"When I'm hungry, I eat; when I'm thirsty, I drink; when tired, I sleep."

During a *sesshin* over which Bankei presided, one of the monks was caught stealing. The other monks brought the matter to Bankei's attention, but he appeared to pay no attention to their complaint. When the offending monk was caught stealing a second time, the monks all went to see Bankei and announced that if he did not expel the thief they would leave the *sesshin*.

Bankei told them: "You're welcome to go elsewhere if you feel you must. But consider the case of this poor monk. Unlike the rest of you, he doesn't even know the difference between right and wrong. If I don't keep him on as a student and teach him, who will?"

The thief was said to have burst into tears when he heard Bankei's words, and he never stole again.

"I have a short and violent temper," a man told Bankei. "It gets me into endless problems, but what can I do? I've always had it. Can you suggest anything?"

"That's a very interesting thing to have," Bankei said. "And you say you've always had it. Can you show me this temper right now?"

"Well, no. I'm not in bad temper just at the moment."

"So when could you show it to me?"

"It isn't like that," the man tried to explain. "It comes up un-expectedly. I can't say when it will rise; I just know it will."

"So it's not something you've always had after all, is it? It isn't part of your true nature, but rather something you work yourself into when certain situations come about. It's due to your partial-ity for yourself. When that partiality is challenged, that's when your temper arises, isn't it? You seek to assert yourself or defend beliefs to which you've become attached. But what would happen if you had no attachments—not even an attachment to self? What cause would there be then for this temper to arise?"

A monk from the Tendai School came to see Bankei. Bankei asked him what practice he pursued.

"I chant the Lotus Sutra," the monk replied.

"Who chants the sutra?" Bankei asked.

"The one who speaks the words."

"Who speaks the words?"

"Eyes horizontal, nose vertical," the monk said smugly, quot-ing Dogen.

"That's mere parroting," Bankei snapped. "Tell me, *who* speaks the words?"

Bankei's *sesshin* were not as formal as those of other teachers. The monks sat zazen or did *kinhin* (walking meditation) when they felt like it. The other trappings of formal meditation retreats were dispensed with, including the *kyosaku*, or "encouragement stick" with which monks in other monasteries were struck when their attention wandered. At one of these retreats, a monk dozed off during one of the meditation periods, and a fellow monk struck him with the *kyosaku* to wake him.

"Why strike him just because he's napping?" Bankei asked. "Do you imagine he leaves the Buddha-mind and goes elsewhere when he's asleep?"

A layman complained about the difficulty he had when trying to meditate. "My mind is constantly filled with thoughts. No sooner do I get rid of one than another arises. How can I clear my mind of these?"

"To try to rid the mind of thoughts by effort is like trying to wash away blood with more blood. What you must realize is the Unborn Buddha-mind is free of illusion. It's because you think your thoughts are something real that you're caught up in them. Just understand that they're unreal, ephemeral apparitions that arise and pass away. Don't seize them or reject them; let them be. They're like the images reflected in a mirror. The mirror itself is empty but reflects whatever is placed before it. Nor does the image leave a stain on the mirror. When the object is removed, the mirror is empty and bright once again. The Unborn Buddha-mind is much brighter than any mirror."

On another occasion, a man complained: "Some time ago, I asked you how to deal with the thoughts that arise in my mind, and you told me to just let them rise and pass by without bothering about them. Well, I've tried that, and nothing happens! My mind is still beset with thoughts from the time I wake until I lay down at night, and then it is filled with dreams!"

"Your problem is that you believe there's some technique to be used which will make your thoughts cease," Bankei told him.

When word went out that Bankei had fallen ill in 1693, disciples from all around Japan rushed to see him one last time. He remonstrated with them, telling them, "If you think of me in terms of birth-and-death, then you don't know me at all." He refused to compose the traditional death poem, saying that he had been a practitioner of the Buddha way for forty-five years and that was testament enough.

Although Suzuki Shosan's martial Zen stands in stark contrast to Bankei's much more gentle teaching, they both sought to bring Zen out of the monastic environment and into the lives of ordinary people. For this they would be criticized by the hierarchies of the traditional schools. Hakuin, for example, insisted that Bankei's Zen was far too lenient to be effective. Still he remains a popular figure in the Zen tradition, in no small part because the Zen he taught is accessible to both the religious and the laity.

Portrait of Matsuo Basho

CHAPTER FOURTEEN

THE POET

Matsuo Basho

Joso

Matsuo Basho

Japanese Zen found its purist poetic expression in the work of Matsuo Basho, just as Chinese Zen had found its in the poems of Hanshan and Shide [cf. *Zen Masters of China*, Chapter Ten]. Although Basho was a formal student of Zen for only a short time, his work is infused with Zen sensibility, and the tradition has adopted him as its own.

He was born in 1644 to a samurai family of modest means. His father died when Basho was twelve years old, and the boy was placed as a servant in the household of the local Daimyo, Todo Yoshitada. Yoshitada was only a few years older than his young servant, and they discovered they had similar tastes. It was Yoshitada who introduced Basho to poetry, in particular to *renga* and *haiku*.

Renga is a complex poetic form in which each member of a group of poets takes turns composing alternate stanzas of three lines (of five, seven, five syllables) or two lines (both of seven syllables). Each pair of stanzas, compromising five lines, needs to be able to stand alone; in this manner, each individual stanza forms the last lines of one five line group and simultaneously the first lines of a second group. Part of the interest in the form is the way in which the meaning of each individual stanza changes depending upon the stanza with which it is paired. The term for the opening stanza is *hokku*; it is the only stanza that needs to be able to stand by itself. It was from this opening stanza that *haiku* as an independent art form evolved.

Although Basho would come to be considered a master of the *haiku* form, he was more proud of his abilities as the leader of *renga* compositions, a role he played throughout his life.

Yoshitada had some formal training under the poet, Kitakura Kigin, better known by his *nom de plume*, Sengin, and Basho may also have studied with him as well. Yoshitada was not a serious poet; what he engaged in with Basho was a literary pastime popular with the upper classes. Participants vied in demonstrating wit and clever word play; they made frequent allusions to the classical literatures of China and Japan. The young nobles who took part in these compositions were dilettantes. Both Yoshitada and Basho, however, were talented enough by the standards of the day that samples of their *haiku* were published in an anthology brought out in 1664.

Yoshitada died in 1666, to be succeeded by his brother, who shared neither his interest in poetry nor his affection for the young retainer who was more concerned about literary than military matters. Basho surrendered his samurai status and left the household to travel to Kyoto where he hoped to acquire an education that would allow him to earn a position in the civil service.

There may have been another reason he left the Todo household. He had been engaged in a number of love affairs as a young man—including, it was rumored, one with Yoshitada's wife. It was not uncommon for samurai to engage in homosexual relations, and Basho admitted that he experimented with these as well although his natural inclination was heterosexual. His longest relationship was with a Shinto nun named Jutei who bore him at least one child.

His academic training in Kyoto was traditional; he studied calligraphy and classical literature. He also continued to pursue poetry under the guidance of Nishiyama Soin, whose style Basho followed until he developed his own.

Upon the formal completion of his studies in 1672, he went to Edo where he found a position in the municipal waterworks. It was not a job likely to have held his interest. Soon the security associated with a civil service position palled, and poetry beckoned. He was a member of several poetic circles, and his work was published regularly. Eventually his reputation was strong enough that he was able to set himself up as a *haiku* instructor. Slowly he gathered a group of students. These were so fond of their teacher that they built him a small home in the suburbs of Edo and planted a banana tree (*basho*) in the front garden to provide shade. The poet called the hut *Bashoan*, Banana-tree Hermitage, and it was from this that he acquired the name by which he is known to posterity.

By the time he was in his mid-thirties, he had established a unique style and was a widely admired poet. His work displayed a deep love for and understanding of nature.

> A cicada shell
> It sang itself
> Away

He had both students and patrons, and, physically, his life was comfortable; however, he also felt a deep dissatisfaction. Then his small hut was destroyed by a fire which swept through his neighborhood, leaving him homeless; shortly afterwards, he received word that his mother had died.

A growing awareness of the transience of life drove him to seek instruction in Zen. The teacher he found, at nearby Komponji, was named Butcho. Basho briefly considered becoming a monk; but in the end he did not have his head shaved, and he remained a layman. He did, however, commit himself seriously to the practice of zazen under Butcho's direction.

Over and over Butcho would challenge Basho to express his understanding of Buddhism, and the student would reply by quoting sutras he had read while a student in Kyoto or by making reference to Chinese or Japanese Zen masters of the past.

"These are the words of others," Butcho chided him. "Let me hear your words."

In spite of his prowess as a poet, Basho had no reply. Then one day, Butcho passed by the monastery pond where Basho was engaged in meditation. "How is your practice proceeding?" he inquired.

Basho automatically answered poetically. "After the rains, the grass is greener than ever."

"So," Butcho shot back, "tell me of the nature of Buddhism before the greenness of the grass."

Basho was stymied for a moment. Then the event took place that brought him to awakening. There was a splash in the pond. "A frog jumps into the water," Basho said. "Hear the sound!"

Later he re-worked this into his best-known koan—which is even briefer in its English rendition than it is in Japanese.

> An old pond
> A frog jumps in
> Water sound!

The hut by the banana tree had been rebuilt while Basho was studying with Butcho, but the poet found himself drawn to homelessness. This led him to undertake the first of several journeys he would make around the island of Honshu. Travel was a difficult activity in the physical and social environment of 17th century Japan, and Basho was not particularly strong physically. He understood that his life could even be in jeopardy during the trip. He warned his disciples that they should not be surprised if he were killed by bandits or expired of exhaustion somewhere along the route. In spite of the dangers, he was committed to the endeavor. He wanted to challenge himself.

His first journey was from Edo to Kyoto and back, by way of his hometown—where his brother presented him with a lock of their dead mother's hair. That prompted this haiku:

If I were to hold it in my hand
It would melt with my tears—
The frost of autumn

Basho's itinerary included sites, such as Mount Fuji, noted for their beauty, as well as famed shrines and temples. The conditions were every bit as difficult as he had expected. He stayed in inns when they were available and in stables or other rough circumstances when they were not. He caught the flavor of these in another haiku:

Lice, fleas
A horse pissing
By my pillow

An example of the harshness of both the social and economic conditions was expressed in an early passage in the journal he kept of the trip. Beside a flooded river he came upon a small child, about two years old, who had been abandoned by his parents. Basho described the situation and even composed a haiku on the episode; however, he did not try to rescue the child whom he believed to be doomed by circumstances and fate.

Apparently his parents . . . had decided to leave him there until his life vanished like a dewdrop. He looked like a tiny bush-clover blossom that would fall any time tonight or tomorrow beneath the blow of an autumn gust. I tossed him some food from my sleeve pocket, and mused as I passed by. . . .

How did this happen? Were you hated by your father, or were you shunned by your mother? No, your father did not hate you, nor did you mother shun you. All this has been Heaven's will; you have nothing but your fate to grieve for. (47)

Basho proved to be as skilled in prose composition as he was in verse, and his travel diary was rewritten in Edo and published as *Nozarashi Wo—A Field of Bones Exposed to the Weather.*

Within two years, he was off on another journey. The second was his most satisfying, although the route was almost the same as the first. Now his fame as a poet preceded him wherever he went. In addition he had made friends during the first trip who now welcomed him on his return. He produced two journals from this expedition.

If the second was the most rewarding of his trips, the third—to the north of the island—was the most strenuous and demanding. Basho and his companion, Kawai Sora, traveled 2400 kilometers over a period of 150 days.

His Zen practice had matured by this time, as well as his poetic talents, and he now had a deep sense of having quelled his ego and achieved a sense of participation in the natural order of things. This sense is expressed in one of his most beautiful haiku:

> No one walks
> Along the path
> This autumn evening

He stayed for a while with friends and admirers near Lake Biwa, east of Kyoto, and then returned to Edo in 1691. The Banana-tree

Hermitage had been rebuilt a second time, and it was there that Jutei joined him. She was in poor health and brought several children with her. Now in his later years, Basho found himself suddenly laden with the responsibilities associated with being the head of a busy household. He struggled with these involvements, seeking a way of remaining detached at a time when he was more thoroughly immersed in worldly affairs than at any other period of his life.

In 1694, he undertook his last journey. A popular story mentions a prior trip that he had planned to make in order to view the flowers that were in bloom at a noted locale. Soon after he set out, Basho came upon a group of people talking about the daughter of a peasant family who was noted for the great devotion she demonstrated in the care she provided her aged parents. Basho made a detour to visit this young woman and was so impressed with her that he gave her the money he had saved for the flower viewing expedition. When he returned to Edo, his students asked about the flowers.

"I saw something more beautiful than flowers," Basho told them.

Basho was accompanied on his last trip by one of Jutei's sons, a young man name Jirobei. The poet's health was not good, and, when he got to Osaka, he was unable to continue. His last poem summoned up his condition:

> Ailing on my journey,
> My dreams alone wander
> This desolate moor

Word of his illness reached Edo, and a number of his disciples rushed to Osaka to be with him at the end. He died peacefully surrounded by admirers.

Although Basho is sometimes credited with developing *haiku* into a serious art form, that process had already begun by poets like Matsunaga Teitoku whose work both Yoshitada and the young Basho imitated. Basho's contribution was to free the form from its dependency on word play and literary allusion. His poems were more personal and profound than those of his predecessors and were deeply infused with his love of the natural world. Even in translation, the poems impress the reader with Basho's ability to capture personal experience vividly in such a succinct form.

For Basho, the purpose of poetry was to draw attention to those myriad things in life that most people pass without noticing. The enhanced sensibility of the artist—whether poet, painter, or even tea master—called others to experience life more fully. In his third travel journal he wrote:

> One thing permeates . . . Sogi's linked verse [*renga*], Sesshu's paintings and Rikyu's tea ceremony. This is the spirit of the artist who follows nature and befriends the four seasons. Everything he sees becomes a flower, and everything he imagines turns into a moon. One who does not see the flower is akin to a barbarian, and one who does not imagine the moon is no different from a beast. Leave barbarians and beasts behind. Follow nature and return to nature. (48)

Poetry is always an expression of a specific linguistic heritage with its unique vocabulary—the connotations and etymology as well as the definition of words—pronunciation and cadence. As such, it can seldom be effectively translated into another language. These English renderings of sample haiku, therefore, can only hint at Basho's skill:

Morning glories in bloom
Fasten the gate
Of an old fence

Spring!—
A nameless hill
Seen behind the mist

Clouds of cherry blossoms—
Does this temple bell sound
In Ueno or Asakusa?

A monk drinking morning tea
All is quiet
The chrysanthemums bloom

On a dead branch
A solitary crow perches—
Autumn evening

Under the same roof
Prostitutes are also asleep—
Moonlight and clover

A melancholy fate—
Persons becoming bamboo shoots
After their demise

The last poem was written when Basho visited the grave of a famous Imperial Concubine and found the site overgrown with young bamboo shoots.

Joso

By the time of his death, Basho had more than two thousand disciples, and the nature of *haiku* had changed forever.

One of his disciples the Buddhist monk, Joso, was the protagonist of one of the popular Zen stories collected by the translator, Thomas Cleary, in *Zen Antics*:

> Originally a samurai, Joso was a hereditary retainer of a certain barony. As the eldest son, he was due to inherit his father's estate, but he was devoted to his stepmother and arranged for her son, his younger half-brother, to succeed to the family inheritance instead.
>
> In feudal Japan, it was not possible to make such a decision arbitrarily. Deliberately wounding his right hand, Joso retired from official service on the grounds of disability, claiming he could not wield a sword. Unfit to be a warrior, he was no longer qualified to become head of a samurai house.
>
> That was how the poet Joso freed himself from worldly affairs to become a Zen monk. After the death of his teacher Basho, he secluded himself in a cave for three years, where he wrote out an entire Buddhist scripture on pebbles, one Chinese character to a pebble, and piled them up into a traditional "scripture mound." (49)

Joso compared himself to a snail which abandons its shell, becoming a slug, in order to achieve freedom.

His fear had been
that his moisture would dry up
and now he has the dew of the rain forest.

Painting and haiku by Matsuo Basho

*"Quietly, quietly,
yellow mountain roses fall—
sound of the rapids."*

Chapter Fifteen

SHOJU ROJIN AND HIS DISCIPLE

Dokyo Etan [Shoju Rojin]

Hakuin Ekaku

Dokyo Etan [Shoju Rojin]

Shido Munan's only Dharma successor was Dokyo Etan. As a young man, Etan had been a retainer in the household of Lord Matsudaira Tadatomo of Nagano. His interest in Zen was roused when a number of older samurai asked an itinerant monk to write down the name of the Bodhisattva of Compassion as talismans for their safety. Etan asked for one as well, but the monk recognized something deeper in the young man than he had sensed in the other soldiers.

"The Bodhisattva isn't to be sought without," he told Etan. "These trifles are of no value. Seek the Bodhisattva within."

The monk's words stayed with Etan, and he became preoccupied with seeking to understand what they meant. The matter of the Bodhisattva Within became his Great Doubt, and he focused on it for many months with such intensity that it often distracted him while he was carrying out his assigned duties. One day, he fell from a ladder and was knocked unconscious. When he came to, the question was resolved. He felt certain he now knew what the Bodhisattva Within was, but he wanted to have his understanding confirmed by a Zen teacher.

The opportunity came when he was assigned to be part of Matsudaira's entourage during a visit to Edo. In that city, Etan sought out Shido Munan who told the young samurai that he had had a genuine awakening, but that it needed to be cultivated further. Etan sought permission from his lord to leave his service and became a monk. Matsudaira, himself a devout Buddhist, readily granted the request.

For one year, Etan underwent strenuous training with Munan, after which the teacher gave him a certificate of *inka*. Etan was twenty years old at the time. Munan then encouraged Etan to go on the traditional pilgrimage to other temples in order to deepen his understanding. After he completed his pilgrimage and returned to Edo, he discovered that Munan had ambitions for him that Etan did not share.

According to a popular story, one evening, Munan called Etan to his quarters. The master was seated in front of a brazier of coals that warmed the chilly room. "I'm old," he told Etan, "and you alone of all my disciples have the capacity to carry on my teaching."

Etan bowed in silence, acknowledging Munan's confidence in him.

Munan brought out a manuscript and presented it to the younger man. "This is a text which I received from my teacher, Gudo Toshoku, who received it in turn from his teacher, and so on. I've added some notes in which I express my understanding. It's an important record, and I'm entrusting it to you."

"If it's so important, perhaps you should keep it," Etan said, gently pressing the manuscript back into Munan's hands.

"I want you to have it as evidence that you're my successor," Munan said, once again presenting it to Etan.

"You used no written text when I received your teaching; I don't need one now."

"That's true," Munan admitted, "but the document has been passed from teacher to student for seven generations, so please accept it as a symbol that you're the heir of that teaching."

Munan placed the manuscript in Etan's lap. Etan took it up and tossed it onto the coals of the brazier.

"What are you doing!" Munan shouted, angrily.

"What are you saying!" Etan shouted, just as loudly.

Munan did not give up his intention to install Etan as his successor, and when his disciples raised funds to establish a temple for him, Munan refused to serve as its founding abbot and gave the honor to Etan. Etan, too, turned it down, and hid in his home village until he heard that someone else was appointed to the position.

After remaining with Munan a while longer, Etan retired to a hermitage in the mountains known as Shojuan. His mother, who had become a nun, joined him there. They both lived ascetic lives. He undertook practices such as meditating in cemeteries, in one incident remaining in meditation posture motionless while wild dogs sniffed at his body. Contemporary accounts describe him as going about in a tattered robe with unkempt hair. People called him "The Old Man of Shoju Hermitage" or Shoju Rojin. This is the name he was known by in 1710, when one of his disciples, Doju Sokaku, brought a proud young man named Sugiyama Iwajiro to visit him.

Etan lived eighty years. Just before he died, he assumed meditation posture and took up his brush to write his death poem:

> Hurrying to die,
> It's difficult to find a last word.
> If I spoke the wordless word,
> I wouldn't speak at all!

Then he laid down his brush, chuckled, and passed away.

HAKUIN EKAKU

Sugiyama Iwajiro is now known by his Buddhist names, Hakuin Ekaku. He was born, in 1686, in the small community of Hara in Shizuoka Prefecture on the highway between Kyoto and Edo. It was an impoverished region near the foot of Mount Fuji, and, throughout his life, Hakuin would retain a great empathy for the lower classes of Japanese society.

His father was a samurai of limited means who had been adopted into his wife's family. Hakuin's mother was a devout practitioner of Nichirin Buddhism, an offshoot of Tendai developed by the 14th century Japanese monk after whom the sect was named. Their youngest child was an intellectually gifted boy, but somewhat sickly and over sensitive. His mother began the child's religious formation by telling him stories from the life of the Buddha. He took pleasure in these stories and memorized the *Lotus Sutra*.

When he was about eight years old, his mother took him to a public talk given by an itinerant Nichirin priest. In the sermon, the priest described the Eight Fiery Hells to which the wicked were condemned in order to expiate their sins before their rebirth. His description included details of the torments to which the damned were subjected, such as being immersed in cauldrons of boiling water. Because of his sensitive and emotional temperament, Hakuin also had an inflated sense of his personal failings. The sermon terrified him, and he came away certain he would be doomed to one of those hells when he died.

Not long afterwards, he was having a bath with his mother. When the water grew tepid, she asked the servant to add more wood to the fire heating it. As the water became warmer, young Iwajiro burst into tears. When his mother asked why he was crying, he told her of his fear of being sent to one of the Eight Fiery Hells.

"Even a little bit of hot water hurts!" he wailed. "How could I bear the torments of the Fiery Hells?"

She tried to console him by counseling him to think of the infinite mercies of the Bodhisattva Kannon. The boy took her words to heart and acquired a picture of the Bodhisattva and enshrined it in his sleeping quarters. Regardless, his anxiety remained unassuaged. He had a very literal and naïve faith. Once, when he was reciting the *Lotus Sutra*, he was struck by a passage that promised that if one were to chant a particular mantra with sufficient zeal, one would be exempt from harm by either fire or water. Hakuin chanted the mantra unremittingly for several days; he then tested its efficacy by taking up a heated poker from the hearth and touching it to his thigh. Either the mantra or his zeal failed.

Eventually he decided the only hope he had of avoiding condemnation after death was to become a monk.

After some initial resistance from his parents, Hakuin entered monastic life at the age of 15. His first community was the local Zen temple, Shoinji—which would later become his teaching center. Here Tanrei Soden gave him the Buddhist name "Ekaku:" he would adopt the name "Hakuin" later in life after he returned to Shoinji.

When Tanrei died, Hakuin, still in his teens, left his hometown and went to Daishoji in the neighboring community of Numazu. But monastic life seemed as little able to fulfill the claims attributed to it as had the mantra from the *Lotus Sutra*. Hakuin found the life both dull and sterile.

Then, when he had been a monk for four years, he came across the story of the death of the Chinese Zen Master, Ganto Zenkatsu [Yantou Quanhuo—cf. *Zen Masters of China*, Chapter Sixteen]. The region where the master's temple had been located was overrun by bandits, and, in fear for their lives, all of the monks fled. Ganto alone remained in the temple. When the bandits arrived, they found him seated in zazen. They searched the temple for valuables and, frustrated at not find any, took out their anger by slaying Ganto. It was said that as their swords pierced him, he let out a scream so loud it could be heard for miles around. That scream distressed Hakuin, who wondered of what use Ganto's Zen proved to be in the end. This story, on top of the tedium and sense of futility he already felt, drove him to leave the monastery.

He had some talent as a poet and painter and turned to these to give some sense of direction and meaning to his life. However, he found the artistic life no more satisfying than monastic life had been.

One day, the abbot of the local temple brought all the manuscripts and books of the temple library out into the courtyard and placed them in the sun in order to dry out any dampness they had acquired and rid them of insects. These works represented copies of the major religious texts not only of Buddhism but of Confucianism and Taoism as well. Seeing them all assembled like this, young Hakuin wondered how one determined which of the many spiritual paths available one should follow. He took up a volume by chance; it happened to be a collection of the tales of the great Chinese Zen masters. Allowing it to open at random, he came upon the story of Sekiso Soyen (Shishuang Chuyuan—cf. *Zen Masters of China*, Chapter Seventeen) who had been so committed to the quest for enlightenment that he did zazen day and night without interruption, stabbing himself in the thigh with an awl to stave off drowsiness.

The story made Hakuin feel ashamed of his prior puny efforts. Shortly after this, he learned that his mother had died. His immediate reaction was to travel home in order to pay his respects at her gravesite, but, upon reflection, he decided a more appropriate way to honor her would be to rededicate himself to his Zen practice.

He began a tour of Zen temples, seeking instruction from the various teachers he met, and he had an initial "tongue-tip" taste of awakening upon hearing the chirp of a cricket; it was a shallow experience but spurred him onto greater effort.

At the age of twenty-two, his travels brought him to Eiganji, where he took in a series of public lectures being given by the Rinzai teacher, Shotetsu. Between talks, Hakuin spent his time focused on Joshu's Mu. He became so absorbed in the koan that he felt as if he were frozen in the midst of a glacier. Not a thought remained in his mind save for the constant repetition of *mu . . . mu . . . mu* with each breath. When he sat in on the lectures, the koan continued, and he felt as if he were floating in air.

This condition persisted for several days, and then he chanced to hear the toll of a temple bell. At that moment it was if the ice had shattered or a jade tower had come crashing down. Not only was the question of Mu resolved, so too was the question of Ganto's death.

"*I* am Ganto!" he declared. "Wonder of wonders, there is no birth or death! There is no enlightenment to seek! The 1700 koans are of no value whatsoever!"

His pride, he later confessed, soared up "like a mountain," and he believed that no one for the last three hundred years could possibly have had as profound an awakening as he had experienced. So he was entirely unprepared when he went to Shotetsu to have his awakening acknowledged and Shotetsu refused to do so, expressing some doubt about Hakuin's attainment. Shotetsu did not take students, but he suggested that Hakuin needed to work with a teacher to clarify what he had accomplished.

One of Dokyo Etan's disciples, Doju Sokaku, had also been attending Shotetsu's lectures, and he advised Hakuin to come with him to meet his teacher. So in 1708, the two set out for Shojuan. As they approached, they saw the old master—now known as Shoju—chopping firewood. He welcomed his disciple back and invited the two travelers into his hut. There, Hakuin, following the customary practice, presented the master with a verse in which he summed up his understanding. Shoju looked at the poem briefly then tossed the paper aside, saying, "These are just words. Show me what you know."

Hakuin made a gagging sound and replied, "If I had anything to show you, I would vomit it up."

"Show me how you understand *mu*," Shoju demanded.

"How can one touch it?" Hakuin said,

Shoju reached forward, grabbed Hakuin's nose, and gave it a sharp twist. "*Here* is how one can touch it!"

Hakuin was stunned and did not know how to reply.

"You poor cave-dwelling demon," Shoju said dismissively. "Are you really so easily satisfied with this meager understanding?"

Hakuin's former pride in his attainment withered, and he asked: "What's missing?"

"When Nansen was dying, his disciples asked where he would be a hundred years to come. . ." Shoju began, relating the story of the Chinese master's last conversation with his disciples (cf. *Zen Masters of China*, Chapter Eleven). Before he could go any further, Hakuin put his hands over his ears and rushed from the room.

"You cave-dwelling demon!" Shoju called out after him.

Hakuin was sufficiently humbled by the experience to remain at the hermitage, meeting with Shoju regularly in the hope of having his awakening confirmed. But each time he presented himself to the old master, Shoju called him as a "cave-dwelling demon" and sent him on his way.

One evening, Hakuin brought Shoju another verse. Shoju was seated on the veranda of his hermitage enjoying the warm sun after several days of rain. He looked at Hakuin's poem, crumbled it up, saying, "Stuff and nonsense."

"Stuff and nonsense!" Hakuin shouted back at him.

Shoju gripped the lapels of Hakuin's robe in his left hand and beat him with his other fist. Then he threw the startled student off the porch into the mud. Hakuin lay there for a while, stunned, listening to Shoju laugh at him. After a while, Hakuin gathered himself together and rose to his feet. He made his formal bow to Shoju and returned to his quarters.

With renewed vigor, he threw himself into the koan about Nansen's death. One morning sometime later, he was engaged in *takuhatsu* and was so caught up in the koan that he stood in front of one house as if in a trance. The woman of the house watched him with suspicion for a while then rushed out waving her broom at him.

"Go!" she screamed at him. "Go away! Go somewhere else! If you don't go away, I'll hit you!"

He was so absorbed that he ignored her. She hit him with the broom, knocking his hat off, and kept beating him until he fell to the ground unconscious. After the woman returned to her house, a passerby helped Hakuin sit up, patting his cheeks to revive him. When Hakuin came to, he realized he had resolved not only the koan about Nansen's death but several others as well that until that time had puzzled him.

He got to his feet, laughing and clapping his hands in delight. The man who had come to his assistance feared Hakuin was a madman and left him. Hakuin gathered himself together and rushed back to Shoju's hermitage. The master saw him coming and, when Hakuin was within speaking range, shouted at him: "I see something has happened to you. So, tell me about it."

Hakuin described all that had taken place.

"Now you have it!" Shoju told him, and then he assigned his student another koan. He never again referred to Hakuin as a "cave-dwelling demon."

Self portrait by Hakuin Ekaku

CHAPTER SIXTEEN

HAKUIN EKAKU

Hakuin Ekaku is the most celebrated figure in Japanese Zen. His influence was so pervasive that Rinzai Zen came to be known as Hakuin Zen, and virtually all the current Rinzai teachers trace their transmissions back to Hakuin.

Following his awakening, Hakuin remained with Shoju for another eight months. Then Shoju told him it was time to begin gathering his own disciples. Underestimating the impact his student would have, he advised Hakuin to have modest expectations; it would be enough if Hakuin were able to find two or three disciples to continue the tradition.

Hakuin undertook a pilgrimage during which his understanding deepened. Until he was in his forties, he would continue to have further awakenings as well as a number of ecstatic experiences. The impact of these on his physical health, however, was brutal, and he finally collapsed from a nervous breakdown.

He sought medical help without success for a long time. Then he heard of a hermit named Hakuyushi who lived in an isolated cave in the mountains. Hakuyushi was reputed to be trained in Taoist medical theory, including acupuncture and herbal remedies. The cave was not easy to locate, but, with assistance from people in the local community, Hakuin tracked it down.

When he arrived, he found the mouth of the cave covered by a curtain. Somewhat apprehensively, Hakuin drew back the curtain. Inside he found Hakuyushi seated in meditation. Hakuin bowed formally to the hermit and asked permission to enter. Once in, he described his symptoms. Hakuyushi diagnosed his condition as "Zen sickness," which, he explained, came about as the result of successive ecstatic states, as well as having an unhealthy diet and living a sedentary lifestyle. Traditional medical treatments, Hakuyushi said, would not be able to treat such a condition. Instead, he prescribed a treatment that consisted of continued introspection and breathing exercises focused on the *hara* (belly).

Hakuin followed Hakuyushi's instructions, which not only cured him but also maintained him in good health for the remainder of his life.

In 1716, he returned to his home and to Shoinji, which he found in poor repair. It had neither roof nor floor boards. When it rained, Hakuin had to wear a rain hat and high getas (sandals with wooden slats on their soles) even indoors. The land and furnishings were mortgaged to local creditors. Undaunted, Hakuin set about rebuilding it, and subsequently this small rural temple became a center to which students from throughout Japan flocked for the next fifty years. Although Hakuin did not actively seek for disciples, his character was such that genuine aspirants were drawn to him. Word spread throughout the land that a fully enlightened teacher lived in this small community. When Shoinji was no longer able to accommodate all those who sought to work with Hakuin, a number of additional buildings were constructed to house them. He would later have opportunities to become the abbot of larger temples in Edo and Kyoto, but he preferred to remain in Hara.

Although the primary focus of his life's work was on renewing the Rinzai School and in training the monks under his direction, Hakuin also retained a commitment to lay people, in particular the working classes. He took lay disciples and was sensitive to the challenges they faced. While monastic life provided an opportunity for meditators to spend hours each day in formal zazen, lay people, on the other hand, had myriad obligations and responsibilities to which they needed to attend. Hakuin taught them how they could transform their involvements in daily life into opportunities for practice. He wrote poems for the laity that were sung to popular folk melodies. In one of these, an old woman compares the process of becoming aware of true self to grinding corn.

Hakuin even noted that lay people had this advantage: Able to pursue their practice in the midst of the claims of worldly affairs, they had no difficulty when participating in formal monastic retreats. Monks, however, who were able to practice in the solitude and peace of temple life often lost their way when they were thrown into the wider world.

Hakuin returned to art around the age of sixty. He was an accomplished calligrapher and painter, and his work would later inspire Sengai Gibon among others. Hakuin's pieces displayed a great sense of humor and proved to be effective tools in teaching the Dharma to people unable to read.

Hakuin's concern for the laity made him a popular figure with the common people, and he became the subject of many tales. One of the best known of these took place in Hara when he first returned there but before he began to gather students.

The community had welcomed him and honored him as a man of exemplary qualities. One day, however, a neighboring couple discovered that their young daughter was pregnant. They demanded the girl tell them who the father was, and the girl refused to do so. After a while, however, her parents wore her down.

"It's the monk, Hakuin," she said. "He's the baby's father."

The neighbors were outraged. They let it be known far and wide that Hakuin had impregnated the girl, and soon all the good will the populace had had for him evaporated. When the baby was born, the girl's parents took it from her and brought it to Hakuin, telling him: "This is your child. You look after it."

"Is that so?" Hakuin said.

He accepted the baby and did not appear distressed at receiving it. His reputation was in tatters, but he looked after the child to the best of his abilities. He kept it clean and warm, soothed it when it was troubled, and sang it to sleep at night. When he went out begging for food, neighbors provided him milk for the child but little else.

He lived like this for almost a year. Then one winter's day, the girl happened to see Hakuin making his way through the snow, going from house to house, begging for food with the baby tied securely on his back. Seeing him struggle like that, she felt ashamed. She confessed to her parents that it was not Hakuin at all who had fathered the child; rather, it was a young man who worked at the market whom she had been seeing on the sly.

Abashed, her parents rushed to Hakuin and apologized profusely for having discredited him.

"Please, reverend sir, our daughter has agreed to marry this young man, and we beg you to return the child to her."

"Is that so?" Hakuin said, and turned the child over to them.

Another popular story was told of the days when Hakuin was traveling from temple to temple as a youth, before he came to Eiganji but after he had rededicated himself to Zen practice. At one point in his journey, two older monks carrying bundles with their belongings joined him. They were cynical men who, when they noticed how earnest their young companion was, were unscrupulous about taking advantage of him.

One of the men said, "I'm not feeling well, and I've traveled such a long distance. I don't know if I have the strength to continue carrying this bundle."

Hakuin readily offered to carry the bundle as well as his own, and, as he walked, he was so absorbed in his meditation on the koan mu that he was barely aware of the added weight.

Seeing how his partner had fared, the other monk began to moan, "Ah! We've come such a long way, and yet we still have a long journey before us. And I, too, have become ill! Perhaps you could help me as well?"

Hakuin agreed and took up the third bundle. Still focused on mu, he was able to carry all three loads.

Eventually they came to a ferry they needed to board in order to cross a lake. Hakuin laid the three bundles down and settled himself into meditation posture. He was quickly absorbed in a deep samadhi. The weather turned bad, and soon the boat began heaving badly on the rough waters. Although other passengers began to moan in agony, Hakuin persisted in his meditation and eventually, tired from his exertions, drifted gently into asleep. He slept soundly for hours and only awoke after the boat had docked. When he opened his eyes, he was assaulted by the smell of vomit. Looking around, he found that his companions and all the other passengers were lolling about the deck sick because of the turbulent waters they had run into. Hakuin alone had passed the journey unfazed.

As he walked down the gangplank steadily while the rest of the passengers lurched about unsurely, the captain of the ferry remarked, "You're quite the young rascal, aren't you?"

Hakuin was absorbed once more in the koan and went his way.

The father of one of Hakuin's lay disciples was a mean-spirited miser who had no respect for his son's interest in Buddhism. "What profit is there in it?" he demanded.

The disciple came to Hakuin, lamenting his father's avarice. "He will surely be condemned to hell for many years if he doesn't change his way, but what can I do?"

Hakuin said, "Make this suggestion: he should take up the *nembutsu*. Whenever he remembers to do so, tell him to recite it and keep a record of the number of times he does it. At the end of the day, I will pay him one penny for each time he recited it. If he recites one hundred times, I will give him one hundred pennies."

The disciple's father, considering Hakuin a fool, readily accepted the challenge. Day after day, he appeared at Hakuin's hermitage with a book in which he recorded how many times he had recited the name of Amida Buddha, and each day, Hakuin gave him a penny for each recitation.

Then one evening, the old man failed to appear. Nor did he come the next day or the day after that. Hakuin asked the young disciple to check on his father. The boy found him at home, so deeply engrossed in the *nembutsu* that all thoughts of avarice had left his mind.

There was a mad monk who declared to any who would listen to him that he was a fully enlightened Buddha. He tore up copies of the sutras and used them as toilet paper, which scandalized some of Hakuin's students. "Is there nothing you can do about this?" they asked. Hakuin agreed to talk to the mad monk.

"I hear that you use copies of the sutras to wipe your ass," he told the monk.

"I do," the monk said, flatly. "I'm a Buddha. What better paper to use to wipe my ass than the sutras?"

"Ah, a Buddha! Then you are mistaken. A Buddha's ass certainly deserves only the purest and cleanest white paper."

A certain great Daimyo came to visit Hakuin. All Hakuin had to offer his guest by way of refreshments were some cakes made of millet such as the poorest farmers ate. The lord looked at the roughly formed cakes and declined them.

"Take one," Hakuin commanded him. "Eat it and experience the misery of the common people."

An old woman attended one of Hakuin's public talks. She was a devotee of Amida Buddha, also known as the "Buddha of Infinite Light"—the Buddha to whom the *nembutsu* was addressed. Although Hakuin questioned the value of the *nembutsu* for Zen monks, he believed it was a suitable and valuable practice for the laity as long as it was properly understood.

"What use is it to seek the Buddha of Infinite Light outside of yourselves?" Hakuin asked his audience. "If you chant the *nembutsu* in hopes of being reborn in the Pure Land which you imagine to be somewhere other than where you are right now, what use is your practice? Do you know what 'Buddha' means? It means 'the Awakened One.' When you're awakened, your own mind is the mind of Buddha, and where you are at this moment is the Pure Land. There's no point in seeking the Buddha anywhere else but within your own mind. If you want fish, where do you look? You look in water, because that's where fish are found. It's useless to look for them anywhere else. If you want to find the Buddha, seek him in your own mind. There's nowhere else to find him, and, when you do find him, you'll discover that the Infinite Light of the Buddha enlightens everything about you."

The old woman thought, "That doesn't sound so hard. I'll search for the Buddha within and find his light."

So she returned to her home, and focused on the *nembutsu* day and night. As she did her housework, as she gathered fuel wood, as she prepared meals, she kept chanting, "*Namu Amida Butsu!*"

After many months of this, she was washing a pot one day and had a sudden awakening. She rushed to see Hakuin.

"The light of Buddha shines through everything!" she declared.

"Is that so?" Hakuin said. He pointed to some animal droppings alongside the road. "What about that pile of shit? Does it shine through that?"

The old woman slapped him and said, "You mean you don't really understand?"

Hakuin burst out laughing.

At the end of December, 1768, Hakuin felt ill. A physician was called in who, after examining him, determined that there was nothing seriously wrong with the old man. After the doctor left, Hakuin remarked, "He was certainly a quack; he couldn't even recognize someone who'll be dead within a matter of days."

One day the following month, his disciples came to his quarters in Shoinji and found that he had died in his sleep. He was 83 years old. His legacy included more than ninety monks to whom he had conferred *inka*.

Hakuin took upon himself the responsibility of affecting a complete reform of the Rinzai School. Central to that reform was ensuring that only individuals who had legitimately received *inka* be allowed to teach. It was essential that students work with genuinely awakened teachers, although Hakuin realized there were only a few available in Japan during his lifetime.

He set high standards for both students and teachers. He had no illusions about the difficulties facing those who came to him, but he believed that sincere students would always be found willing to pursue the path regardless of how difficult it was.

Awakening was central to Hakuin's Zen. One was not, in his opinion, a member of the Zen community until one had "seen into one's true nature." He believed that those, such as Suzuki Shosan, who held that awakening was not important did so only because they had not achieved it themselves. He described them as being like one too weak to feed himself but claiming that the reason he was not eating was because the food had spoiled. While Hakuin was respected as a genial and kind man with a great generosity of spirit and compassion, he could work himself into a furor about teachers, like Bankei, who he believed were compromising the Zen tradition.

Hakuin recognized that it was possible to achieve kensho through a number of practices. He often prescribed that lay people recite the *nembutsu*, but he maintained that the most effective route, and the only suitable route for monks, was koan study. He was dubious about the value of the Soto tradition of *shikan taza* and described the monks who engaged in it as being like incense burners in a mausoleum.

Awakening was not something that came about automatically from the practice of zazen or koan study. One's practice had to be entered vigorously, fueled by great faith, great determination, and great doubt. He advised both monks and lay people to ask, "Who sees? Who hears? When walking, when standing, when sitting, or lying down, in all circumstances, whether favorable or unfavorable, who is that sees? Who is it that hears?"

After being taught to concentrate the attention through *susokkan*, students were given a first koan, which in the Rinzai tradition, was usually *Mu!* But Hakuin coined his own koan, which has become the best known of all: "You know the sound of two hands clapping. But, tell me, what is the sound of one hand?" He used the koan with great success, and whenever one of his disciples passed it, Hakuin marked the occasion by presenting the student with an abbot's staff (roughly shaped like a dragon) on which he wrote the date of their awakening.

Miura and Sasaki provide this example of one of Hakuin's sermons in *Zen Dust*:

> My humble advice to you distinguished persons who study the profound mystery of the Buddha-Dharma is this: Your close examination of yourself must be as urgent as saving your own head were it ablaze; your efforts to penetrate into your own original nature must be as tireless as the pursuit of an indispensable thing; your attitude toward the verbal teachings of the Buddhas and patriarchs must be as hostile as that toward a deadly enemy.
>
> In Zen, he who does not bring strong doubt to bear upon the koans is a dissolute, knavish good-for-nothing. Therefore it is said: "Underlying great doubt there is great satori; where there is thorough questioning there will be a thoroughgoing experience of awakening."
>
> Do not say: "Since my worldly duties are many and troublesome, I cannot spare time to solidify my doubt firmly," or, "Since my thoughts are always flying about in confusion, I lack the power to apply myself to genuine concentration on my koan."
>
> Suppose that, among the dense crowds of people in the hurly-burly of the market place, a man accidentally loses two or three pieces of gold. You will never find anyone who, because the place is noisy and bustling or because he has dropped his pieces of gold in the dirt, will not turn back to look for them. He pushes any number of people about, stirs up a lot of dust, and, weeping copious tears, rushes

around searching for his gold. If he doesn't get it back into his own two hands, he will never regain his peace of mind. Do you consider the priceless jewel worn in the hair, your own inherent marvelous Tao, of less value than two or three pieces of gold? (50)

After an initial breakthrough, practitioners were then guided through a program of koans, each of which enhanced the student's original understanding, a process that could take ten years or more. Hakuin knew from his own experience that the initial kensho could mislead one into believing one was fully awakened. In reality, he taught, after the first kensho one was like a newborn child: one has all one's faculties, but those faculties still need to be cultivated.

Students took part in frequent face-to-face interviews called *sanzen* (*dokusan* in the Soto tradition) during which Hakuin challenged them to show their understanding of the koan on which they were working. Even after completing the course of koans, Hakuin advised students to go over them all again and again.

The systemization of koan work Hakuin developed is still in use today both in Japan and the West, and the poem he wrote in praise of zazen continues to be chanted in Zen centers around the world.

From the beginning all beings are Buddha.
Like water and ice, without water no ice,
Outside us no Buddhas.

How near the truth, yet how far we seek,
Like one in water crying "I thirst."
Like a child of rich birth
wand'ring poor on this earth,
we endlessly circle the six worlds.
The cause of our sorrow is ego delusion.
From dark path to dark path we've wandered in darkness,
How can we be free from the wheel of samsara
    [birth and death]?

The gateway to freedom is zazen samadhi,
beyond exultation, beyond all our praises,
the pure Mahayana.
Observing the precepts, repentance and giving,
the countless good deeds and the way of right living
all come from zazen.
Thus one true samadhi extinguishes evils;
it purifies karma, dissolving obstructions.
Then where are the dark paths to lead us astray?
The pure lotus land is not far away.
Hearing this truth, heart humble and grateful,
to praise and embrace it, to practice its wisdom,
brings unending blessings, brings mountains of merit.

But if we turn inward and prove our True-nature,
that True-self is no-self,
our own Self is no-self,
we go beyond ego and past clever words.
Then the gate to the oneness of cause and
    effect is thrown open.
Not two and not three, straight ahead runs the Way.
Our form now being no-form,
in coming and going we never leave home.

Our thought now being no-thought,
our dancing and songs are the voice of the Dharma.
How vast is the heaven of boundless samadhi!
How bright and transparent the moonlight of wisdom!
What is there outside us, what is there we lack?
Nirvana is openly shown to our eyes.
This earth where we stand is the pure lotus land,
And this very body, the body of Buddha. (51)

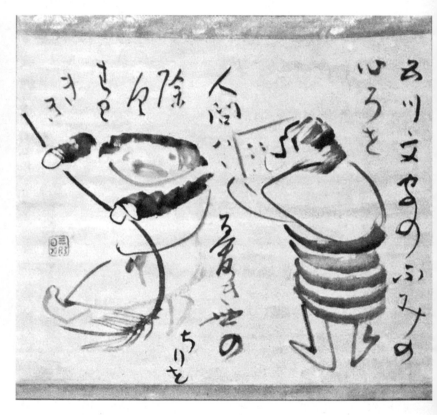

"Kanzan and Jittoku" by Sengai Gibon

CHAPTER SEVENTEEN

HAKUIN'S HEIRS

TOREI ENJI

GASAN JITO

INZAN IEN

TAKUJU KOSEN

TOREI ENJI

When Torei Enji was only five years old, the celebrated Zen Master, Kogetsu Zenzai, visited the boy's family. The child was so impressed with Kogetsu that he expressed a desire to become a monk. His parents dismissed this as a childhood enthusiasm that they expected him to outgrow. When he failed to do so, however, they allowed him to have his head shaved at the age of nine, although it would not be until he was seventeen that he took full ordination.

Under Kogetsu's instruction, Torei achieved an initial kensho; after which, he undertook the traditional pilgrimage to test and deepen his awakening. He did not feel called to remain very long at any of the temples he visited until, in 1743 at Kogetsu's suggestion, he traveled to Shoinji to meet Hakuin.

Until his first encounter with Hakuin, Torei had had no doubt about the genuineness and depth of his awakening, but, when he met Hakuin face-to-face, he could not even open his mouth. Clearly Hakuin's attainment far surpassed his own, and he asked the master to instruct him.

"If a demon were to rise up just now to throw you into Hell," Hakuin challenged him, "how would you free yourself?"

Torei had no idea of how to reply to the question. He joined Hakuin's disciples and applied himself to further zazen. Each time he came to Hakuin in *sanzen*, the master asked if he had yet found a way to free himself, and, for a long while, he had nothing to say. Eventually Torei was able to respond to the koan to Hakuin's satisfaction, but the old master warned him he still had room for further development and should not relax his efforts.

Torei stayed with Hakuin until he received word from his family that his mother had fallen ill, and they requested he return to his hometown to care for her. He did so for two years. After her death, he did not immediately return to Shoinji but went, instead, to Kyoto. There he retired to a hermitage and undertook a rigorous and ascetic training schedule. He had learned from Hakuin that an initial awakening almost always required further deepening, and, to that end, he committed himself to maintain this schedule for one hundred fifty days. After the first one hundred, he felt as if he had reached the end of his resources, but then he rallied and pushed forward:

> —I whipped the dead ox again to forge ahead nonstop. Gritting my teeth and clenching my fists, I didn't notice I had a body. Even on freezing days and frigid nights my clothing was always moist with sweat. Sometimes when the demon of sleep was strong I stuck myself with a needle. Penetrating bone and marrow, finding no taste in food and drink, I passed another half a hundred days. During that time I had insights eight or nine times, and on the last day I saw through my teacher's experience. Ah, ha, ha! The dead work I had mistakenly been doing, along with the white clouds, deserved thirty strokes of the cane. I knew in truth my teacher's empowerment was tremendous—if he hadn't led me along and instructed me so much, how could I be where I am today? I would have spent my whole life mistakenly remaining dead within understanding and knowledge. Now as I think of past events, every word, every phrase, was dripping with blood, frightening and saddening. Ever since then, my mindfulness has been uninterrupted. I studied day and night, never stopping. How can we waste time idly with an easygoing attitude? (52)

He came away from this effort with a profound experience, but one of the reasons his clothing had been damp with sweat even on "freezing days and frigid nights" was that he had succumbed to tuberculosis. He was only thirty years old, but, weakened by both disease and the physical austerities to which he had subjected himself, he was uncertain he would survive his illness. He did not, however, want to die without repaying Hakuin by passing on what he had learned from him. So he undertook to write a guide for new Zen practitioners. The work was entitled *A Discourse on the Inexhaustible Lamp of Zen* [*Shumon Mujinto Ron*], and it provides great insight into the content of the teaching of the Hakuin School.

By the time he had completed the manuscript, Torei's health showed signs of recovery, which left him uncertain what to do with the text. He sent a copy to Hakuin, explaining that he had feared the document might be his only legacy to the Zen School, but now he was unsure whether there was any merit in it and was tempted to burn it. Hakuin wrote back to assure him that the *Discourse* would have a salutary effect on future generations and that he should preserve it.

Torei begins the *Discourse* by defining what distinguishes the Zen School from other forms of Buddhism. It is not that these other schools are in error but that they are inadequate. They are only able to discuss and theorize about awakening but are incapable of bringing people to awakening. These schools teach "the beginning and the end" of the path, whereas Zen points beyond the path to awakening itself. He compares the difference to that between a poor man and a rich man; the poor man can discuss the rich man's wealth, but he cannot make use of it. "So then, of what use is it to him?" Torei asks.

One must undertake Zen practice with proper intent and motivation. The path is difficult and requires persistence, therefore one needs to be properly grounded before proceeding. For Torei, the correct way to do this is through making a whole-hearted commitment to the four vows. These vows, originally formulated in Chinese, were chanted daily in Zen Temples:

> All beings, without number,
>   I vow to liberate.
> Endless blind passions,
>   I vow to uproot.
> Dharma gates, beyond measure,
>   I vow to penetrate.
> The Great Way of Buddha,
>   I vow to attain. (53)

The Four Vows, Torei asserts, are based on compassion. One must undertake the practice of Zen for the benefit of all beings; to do otherwise is to practice in vain. The way in which the Zen aspirant fulfills these vows is by committing him or herself to equal the attainments of the Buddhas and Patriarchs of the past and then to pass that attainment on to "one or two" others.

Nor can one undertake the way on one's own. It requires the guidance of a fully awakened teacher. Torei admits that it is difficult to find such a teacher in these "degenerate times," and he laments the number of unqualified teachers whose inadequate instruction only misleads their students. But without a qualified teacher, students are susceptible to shallow understanding and misleading visions. He compares proceeding without a teacher to setting out on a journey to a distant land without a knowledgeable guide; one has a particular destination in mind, but, because one lacks proper guidance, one may end up somewhere altogether different than where one had intended to be.

While the teacher is necessary, one must also recognize that the path is not an external one. What one is seeking cannot be had from another but can only be found by turning inward. Buddha-nature is not found by learning a doctrine but by searching one's own mind. The basis of this practice is Right Mindfulness, which in turn is cultivated through Right Meditation (zazen). The various regulations associated with monastic life are solely intended to promote Right Mindfulness.

If one practices under appropriate guidance and with correct intention, one will develop a capacity for concentration so strong that conscious thought comes to an end. This, Torei tells us, is the Entrance to the Great Way; when this is attained, one must proceed with care. One must persist without seeking anything in particular; because to do otherwise would be to seek only for something one has imagined. If one can let go of both body and mind, one will come to awakening, the understanding of one's True Nature and the nature of all Being.

Paraphrasing the instructions given by the Sixth Patriarch to General Ming [cf. *Zen Masters of China*, Chapter Three], Torei challenges the student: "Without thinking 'yes' or 'no,' tell me: *Who* is it that sees? *Who* is it that hears? If one persists in this manner, the answer will arise of itself at the appropriate time without the need of discriminating dualistic thought."

Torei goes on to warn the student not to suppose his or her efforts are complete with an initial kensho. From his own experience, as well as that of Hakuin, he understands the importance of "Progressive Enlightenment," and he cites examples of masters from the past whose initial awakenings were deepened by continued practice after kensho. Even if one were to attain a degree of insight equal to that of Bodhisattva Manjusri—the Bodhisattva of Prajna (Wisdom)—one would still be called to continue one's practice in order to integrate awakening into all aspects of one's life.

Torei provides further examples of teachers who, after receiving *inka*, delayed accepting students until they had allowed time for their awakening to mature. Even then, they remained selective about the students they accepted, choosing only those who were able to demonstrate a genuine commitment to strive for awakening.

Although he would continue to suffer from the vestiges of tuberculosis for the remainder of his life, Torei made a strong recovery and began a teaching career that continued for forty years. He returned to Shoinji briefly, where Hakuin presented him with his robe, signifying that he recognized the younger man as his principle Dharma heir.

Torei could have been appointed abbot of a number of temples, but chose not to accept any of these opportunites until Hakuin purchased an old neglected temple, Ryutakuji, in the foothills of Mount Fuji and presented it to him. It was in an area celebrated for its natural beauty, and Torei finally settled there. Hakuin also purchased Shido Munan's hermitage in Edo in order to prevent the government from confiscating the grounds. Torei made use of this as his residence whenever his teaching brought him to the capital city.

In the years that followed, Torei worked with Hakuin to develop a revised curriculum of koan study; the system they devised is still in use both in Japan and the West.

The relationship between Hakuin and Torei went beyond that of master and disciple and became a deep friendship. In Torei, Hakuin found an heir whom he could trust, and, as Hakuin's energy waned in his later years, Torei assumed responsibility for the formation of the students at Shoinji.

On one occasion, a student asked Torei, "Is it true that seeing into one's True Nature is the same as attaining Buddhahood?"

"It is."

"Then you, Master, are a Buddha?"

Torei nodded his head.

"But we've been taught," the student went on, "that Buddhas have special spiritual powers. If you're a Buddha, why don't you have special powers?"

"I most certainly have spiritual powers," Torei replied.

"Then why don't you manifest them so others can see them and be aware of them?"

"I'm always manifesting them. You, however, don't recognize them. It isn't the fault of the sun or the moon if a blind man is unable to see them.

"If, on the other hand, what you're asking about are miracles or magical effects, even if he attains these abilities, a true teacher wouldn't make use of them. Because if he should, people would come to believe, 'This is a man of exceptional qualities; we can't hope to achieve what he's achieved.' In that way they would fail to discover their own spiritual powers."

After Hakuin's death, Torei left Shoinji and retired to Ryutakuji. He worked on restoring the old buildings, transforming the temple into a center worthy of the beauty of its location. He remained there for twenty years. In his seventies, he returned to a small temple in his hometown, where he died in 1792.

GASAN JITO

Gasan Jito was one of Hakuin's later students who completed his training under Torei Enji's tutelage.

He had begun his studies with Gessen Zenne, who was a Dharma successor of Kogetsu Zenzai. The records of the Hakuin School portray Gessen as a rival of Hakuin, perhaps jealous of the more famous teacher's popularity. Several of Gessen's students, like Gasan, would go on to work with Hakuin. However, Gessen was an accomplished Zen master whose Dharma heirs included Sengai Gibon.

Gasan achieved an initial kensho while with Gessen, then undertook the traditional pilgrimage to other temples. None of the masters he visited, however, had anything more to teach him, and he returned to Gasan, convinced that he was now fully awakened. Gasan concurred and told Gessen that he had no further need to test his understanding.

Gasan remained with his teacher for a while longer before it occurred to him that the one Zen Master he had not yet visited was Hakuin Ekaku. He mentioned the matter to Gessen, but Gessen assured him there was no need to visit Hakuin. So Gasan did not pursue the matter any further. About a year later, however, Hakuin was giving a series of lectures in Edo, and Gasan attended one out of curiosity. He was so impressed with what he heard that he took formal leave of Gessen and traveled to Hara in order to study with Hakuin.

During their first interview, Gasan intended to present Hakuin with his understanding of the Dharma, but, after only a few words, Hakuin laughed derisively and demanded, "What charlatan has deluded you so much that you feel qualified to come here and foul the air with your breath?" Then he thrust Gasan from the room.

Twice more Gasan sought admission to Hakuin's community of monks, and twice more the old man sent him away.

Through all of this, Gasan had maintained his belief that what he had achieved under Gessen's guidance had been genuine and complete awakening. He supposed that Hakuin was only refusing to acknowledge the fact as some form of test. After being dismissed the third time, however, he reflected that a teacher of Hakuin's reputation would not behave as he was without good cause.

On the next occasion he met with Hakuin, Gasan began by apologizing for presuming to present himself as an awakened individual and humbly asked for Hakuin's instruction.

"What you have is genuine enough," Hakuin told him, "but it is still only a tongue-tip taste of Zen. You still need to hear the sound of one hand clapping."

For the next four years, Gasan applied himself to zazen under Hakuin's direction, continuing it under Torei Enji after Hakuin died. It was from Torei that Gasan finally received *inka*.

Gasan became one of the foremost proponents of what was then being called "Hakuin Zen," and he served for a time as abbot of Shoinji. His two most important heirs were Inzan Ien and Takuju Kosen.

Inzan Ien

Inzan Ien's parents sensed that there was something odd about their son from an early age. So when a monk by the name of Rozan Oaho suggested that the child, then nine, already exhibited the qualities of a monk, Inzan's parents rushed to have him ordained.

For seven years, Inzan studied with Rozan then he worked for a while with one of Bankei's heirs. Following that, he spent several years with Gessen Zenne. As had Gasan, Inzan achieved his initial kensho while with Gessen. Then he, too, followed the tradition of traveling from temple to temple to deepen his awakening.

During his travels he found no teacher whose understanding equaled his. Believing there was nothing more for him to learn, he accepted a post as priest of a small, impoverished temple in central Japan. He remained at that temple for ten years, caring for

the devotional needs of the local people and providing accommodations to traveling monks who passed through the region.
One of these monks happened to tell Inzan about Gasan who, the
monk claimed, was recognized by many as the preeminent Zen
Master of the day.

Inzan was intrigued. He went to Edo to see if Gasan's insight
were any deeper than his own. He sought a private interview with
the teacher. Before he could say a word, however, Gasan held his
hand up in front of Inzan's face and demanded, "Tell me, why is
this called a hand?"

Inzan was momentarily baffled but gathered his wits and
started to venture a reply. Gasan cut him off by lifting his leg and
asking, "And why is this called a foot?"

Once again, Inzan tried to respond, but Gasan laughed loudly
and pushed the younger man from the room.

When Inzan returned the following day, Gasan told him:

> People who practice Zen today go through the impenetra-
> ble koans of the ancients breezily, without ever having done
> any real work. They versify the koans, or quote them, or
> add capping phrases, or give answers, all of them running
> off at the mouth, talking at random.
>
> For this reason many of them lose the spirit of the Way
> after they become abbots. Even if they don't run into trou-
> ble, none of them can really be teachers. It is truly pitiful.
>
> If you really want to practice Zen, then cast off every-
> thing you have studied and realized up until now and seek
> enlightenment single-mindedly. (54)

Under Gasan's instruction, Inzan completed the revised koan
curriculum developed by Hakuin and Torei. Then, he achieved
fame as an exponent of the Hakuin School of Zen.

In 1806, he rebuilt Zuiryoji in the city of Gifu and gathered
a number of lay and ordained disciples. Two years later, he was

appointed Abbot of Myoshinji. He served in that capacity for a while then returned to Zuiryoji where he died at age 64.

TAKUJU KOSEN

Takuju Kosen was twenty years old when he came to study with Gasan. The master assigned him Joshu's *Mu!*, and the young man threw himself into the practice. He requested permission to retire from the monastic community to a hermitage in order to dedicate all of his time to the koan. He practiced with such fervor that at one point he went for more than two weeks without either food or sleep. As a result of his efforts, he was able to attain kensho within ninety days.

After completing his training with Gasan, Takuju spent another twenty years in further solitude, deepening and integrating his understanding. Then he succeeded Inzan as abbot of Myoshinji.

Both Inzan and Takuju were effective teachers, but what commentators—such as the American Zen teacher Bernie Glassman—note was the difference in their personalities:

> Inzan and Takuju had completely different personalities. Inzan was vigorous, very dynamic; Takuju was meticulous, very careful in his study. And thus two koan systems developed, having the characteristics of each teacher: one very dynamic, and one system requiring you to be very meticulous in examining all elements of each point of a koan. (55)

The majority of Rinzai teachers today are direct Dharma descendants of one or the other of these two men, making use of the different approaches Inzan and Takuju took to koan study.

"Tea Implements" by Sengai Gibon

CHAPTER EIGHTEEN

SENGAI GIBON AND RYOKAN DAIGU

Sengai Gibon and Ryokan Daigu are two of the most famous Zen figures from the turn of the 18th and 19th centuries. One practiced in the Rinzai tradition, the other in the Soto. One was the 123rd abbot of the oldest Zen Temple on the islands; the other lived in obscurity in a hermitage on Mount Kugami. One achieved so much prominence as a sumi-e painter that he once complained people appeared to have mistaken his quarters for a privy because of the numerous scraps of paper they left there hoping he would grace them with one of his drawings. The other's fame only came posthumously, after his mistress published his poems. What they have in common is that their work expresses—one in painting and the other in verse—the feel of the perspective of the awakened individual.

SENGAI GIBON

Sengai Gibon's parents were farmers, and throughout his life he retained a deep respect for agricultural workers. "Farmers," he wrote, "are the foundation of civilization." He became a monk at age eleven, primarily in order to reduce the financial burden on his family. At the temple school he attended, he was introduced not only to Buddhist doctrine and practice, but also to calligraphy, brushwork, and poetic composition. Even as a youngster, Sengai demonstrated a talent for drawing.

At the age of nineteen, he decided to look for a teacher who could help him achieve awakening. He traveled about Japan, visiting temple after temple, seeking an appropriate master, finally settling upon Gessen Zenne, under whose direction Gasan Jito and Inzan Ien had come to their first kensho.

Gessen assigned Sengai the koan based on a problem Kyogen Chikan put to his disciples [Xiangyan Zhixian; cf. *Zen Masters of*

China, Chapter 14]:

> "Imagine that a man has climbed high into a tree then falls.
> Before he hits the ground, he is able to grab a branch be-
> tween his teeth. There he hangs, his hands unable to grasp
> anything, his feet dangling. A sincere inquirer comes by
> and asks him, 'Why did the First Patriarch come east?' If he
> speaks, he'll fall and die. If he doesn't speak, he fails in com-
> passion by not responding to the question. If you were in
> his circumstances, what would you do?"

When Sengai resolved the koan, he followed the traditional
practice of expressing his understanding in verse:

> Old Shakyamuni has been dead some 2000 years
> Maitreya Buddha will not be born for eons to come
> Sentient beings find this difficult to comprehend
> But this is the way it is: the nostrils above the lips

Sengai remained with Gessen for another thirteen years, until the
master's death in 1781, then he completed koan study with Gessen's successor, Seisetsu Shucho. After that, he undertook a second
pilgrimage of Zen temples before eventually accepting the position of abbot at Shofukuji, the temple founded at Hakata by
Myoan Eisai in 1195. There he acquired a reputation for his prowess as a spiritual director and for his personal modesty. He eschewed
the formal trappings of office and limited his meals to what he
acquired through the daily round of *takuhatsu*. He refused to accept Imperial Honors until it would have been impolitic to continue to do so. When he did finally agree to receive the purple
robe, the sign of the highest rank a priest could achieve, he did

not attend the investiture ceremony himself but sent a proxy. He used the funds intended for the celebration of his promotion on temple repairs

At the age of 61, he appointed his primary Dharma Heir, Tangen Toi, abbot in his stead and he retired to a small hermitage he called Kyohakuin—"The Empty White House."

Freed from the responsibilities of an abbot of a major Zen Temple, Sengai looked forward to a time of solitude and described his new life in a number of poems:

> Buddha had 80,000 monks
> Confucius 3000 disciples.
> I sit alone on a vine-covered stone
> Watching the occasional cloud go by.

This verse accompanies a drawing of Kyohakuin:

> I came alone
> I will die alone
> In between
> I remain alone night and day.
>
> The I who came thus
> The I who will pass away thus
> Is the same I living
> In this small hut all alone.

These poems, however, may have described more an idealistic than an actual state, because, as it turned out, in some ways Sengai's career began after his retirement.

Once he retired to Kyohakuin, he dedicated himself to art. While he had had no professional training other than that which all Rinzai students acquired, he had a prodigious talent, and his work quickly gained admirers. He made use of the same monochromatic sumi-e form that had been used by many Zen-influenced artists, including Hakuin. Sengai's works often consisted of only a few quick brush strokes, at times accompanying a poem or other work of calligraphy, but the almost nonchalant images he composed in this manner were full of vigor and humor. One of his most reproduced paintings consists only of a circle, a triangle, and a square—the three most basic geometrical forms. (See the illustration on page 60; Japanese script is read from right to left, so the image appears reversed to western viewers who see the square, rather than the circle, at the beginning of the sequence). Unlike Ikkyu, Sengai was scrupulous about keeping the precepts and generally led an exemplary life, but at times his humor was as racy as Ikkyu's—as in a painting of a priest's penis with the inscription, "An unused treasure."

Almost anything he saw inspired him. His subjects included landscapes, people engaged in the most mundane activities (such as measuring salt), household implements, animals, and sea life; he drew men working in the fields, their crops, and the tools they used; he made pictures of flowers, bamboo, and reeds. He also, of course, returned over and over to Buddhist themes, including several light-hearted portraits of Bodhidharma, one of which included the inscription: "Nine years seated before a wall—how boring!" He did a number of paintings based on Basho's koan about the old pond and the frog, including some parodies:

> An old pond
> Basho jumps in
> Water sound!

What Sengai demonstrated in his art, what continues to make his pieces so attractive, is the natural playfulness that follows from the Zen experience of awakening. In spite of the rigorous training associated with the practice, it results in a joyous and irreverent sense of being at home in the world. Sengai caught that feeling nicely in his painting of Tanka Tennen [Tanxia Tianran, cf. *Zen Masters of China*, Chapter Six] warming his buttocks on the fire he had made by burning a wooden Buddha.

In spite of his longing for solitude, Sengai found himself besieged with visitors after his retirement. His personal friends included poets, tea-masters, artists, musicians, as well as local merchants, craftspeople, and medical practitioners. There was also a local drunk, Icimaru Iwane, whose caricature Sengai drew bringing him a pot of turnips, "to try to trick me into doing a drawing for him."

Some of his visitors came for spiritual guidance, but many, like Icimaru, came to ask for one of his calligraphies or a drawing. People brought bits of paper, hoping he would write a few words or make a quick sketch, prompting his remark that perhaps they mistook Kyohakuin for a privy. This stream of visitors could be exhausting, and on one occasion, Sengai stuck his head out his window and shouted, "The abbot is away today! Please come back another time!"

When Sengai was first appointed Abbot of Shofukuji, he discovered that some of the monks were in the habit of sneaking out of the monastery at night in order to spend time in bars and brothels. One monk in particular made regular forays in this manner.

Sengai found the small wooden platform the monk had been placed against the wall to assist him in leaving and returning to the temple grounds. One night, when he knew the monk was engaged on another of these excursions, Sengai removed the platform and waited by the wall. On his return home the monk mounted the wall and extended his foot towards the platform. He stepped instead into the cupped hands of the abbot. Sengai carefully helped him down, then, without a word of admonition, told the monk, "It's a very damp morning; please take care not to catch cold."

The platform was never replaced, and monks no longer snuck out of the monastery at night.

After achieving his initial kensho, Tangen Toi asked Sengai permission to undertake the traditional pilgrimage to other temples to deepen his understanding. But each time he put in his request, Sengai wordlessly gave him a rap on the head with his abbot's stick. After being refused in this way several times, Tangen approached the head monk and asked if he would intervene on his behalf. The head monk agreed to do so and spoke to Sengai who relented and agreed to allow Tangen to begin his journey. However, when Tangen presented himself to thank his teacher, once more Sengai struck him and said nothing.

Tangen sought out the head monk and complained, "I thought you'd said that the master had agreed to allow me to go on pilgrimage. And yet when I saw him just now, once again all he did was strike me. Has he changed his mind?"

The head monk went in to Sengai and asked about the matter.

"Of course Tangen is free to go," Sengai said. "But when he returns he'll be fully awakened, and I won't have any further reason to strike him. I just wanted to take advantage of this last opportunity."

During a New Year's celebration, a group of villagers came to Sengai and asked him to write something in calligraphy that they could hang in their local temple to promote prosperity throughout the coming year. Sengai wrote three lines:

> Parents die
> Children die
> Grandchildren die

"But this is horrible!" the villagers complained.

"Not at all," Sengai told them. "What would be horrible were if things occurred in the other order—if children died before their parents. There's no greater example of good fortune than that things should proceed in their appointed order."

A certain daimyo was so proud of the chrysanthemums growing on his estate that members of his household came to feel he cared more for his flowers than he did for them. When one of his retainers inadvertently broke one of these flowers from its stalk, the daimyo flew into a rage and had the man put under restraint. The retainer, in turn, considered that he had no option but to commit seppuku.

One of the retainer's family members sought out Sengai and asked if there were any way he could intervene on behalf of the imprisoned man. Sengai agreed to see what he could do.

That evening the daimyo heard a commotion in the garden. Rushing out, he found the famous and respected Zen master cutting the blossoms off each of his chrysanthemum stalks. "What's the meaning of this?" the lord demanded.

"Even the most beautiful weeds become rank if they aren't properly pruned," Sengai told him.

The daimyo released his retainer and no longer gave his flowers more consideration than they were due.

Sengai was proud of Shokfukuji's status as a leading Zen temple in Japan, and felt that he left it in good hands when Tangen became abbot. He was happy that Tangen had the opportunity to oversee the temple's 600th Anniversary Celebrations. But, in 1836, Tangen fell afoul of the local authorities and was banished to Oshima Island, and, at age 86, Sengai had to come out of retirement and resume his duties at Shofukuji.

He lived for two more years, attaining the *beiju*—his 88th year, which is considered to be the age of congratulations. He might have lived longer had he not been burdened by the administrative duties of his office. As it was, he fell ill a few weeks after his birthday celebration.

When Sengai was on his deathbed, many of his disciples gathered about to spend his last moments with him. He looked around at them and said, "I don't want to die."

The students considered what he meant by these words, what final message their master intended them to understand. Sengai listened to the discussion for a few moments, then shouted: "No! Really! I don't want to die!"

His death poem was:

> One who knows the where and when of coming
> One who knows the where and when of departing
> No longer clinging to the cliff
> Clouds never know where the breeze will carry them

RYOKAN DAIGU

Ryokan was born in 1758 in a small fishing village called Izumo-zaki about halfway along the mountainous west coast of Honshu. It was a community remote from the cultural and political centers of the country. His father, Tachibana Inan, was the village head-man and a Shinto priest; he was also a poet and had a slight reputation as a composer of haiku. By the standards of the village, the family was fairly well off.

Ryokan was the eldest son, and the probable successor to his father. He was a very social young man, fond of sake and women. But as he neared his 18th birthday, he became more introspective, and, in 1777, to the surprise of his family, he entered Koshoji, the local Soto Temple.

He had been at Koshoji for about four years when the Zen master Kokusen paid a visit to the temple. Ryokan felt drawn to this teacher and returned with him to his temple, Entsuji, in Tama-shima. Ryokan worked with Kokusen for twelve years, studying Zen as well as calligraphy and verse composition. Around this time, he adopted the name Daigu, which means "Great Fool." It was the name by which he most frequently referred to himself.

In 1790 Kokusen presented Ryokan with a certificate of *inka* that read:

> To Ryokan, good as foolish, who walks the broadest way
> So free and so untrammeled, none can truly fathom him.
> I grant this certificate with a stick of mountain wood.
> Everywhere he will find quiet rest as inside the walls. (56)

After Kokusen's death, Ryokan embarked on the traditional pilgrimage, never to return to a monastic community. In 1795, he learned that his father had committed seppuku in Kyoto as an act of protest against the Shogunate and in support of the Imperial Household. Ryokan traveled to the city to perform the memorial rites for his father, then returned to Izumozaki, where his younger brother, Yoshiyuki, was now recognized as the head of the family.

Ryokan found an old hermitage on nearby Mount Kugami, to which he gave the name Gogoan. A *gogo* was half a *sho*, the measure of rice considered necessary to sustain an adult male. True to the name of his residence, he lived there in poverty.

Although he chose to dwell in a hermitage, Ryokan continued to be very social. He came into the village frequently to beg for food or to spend time drinking at the inn with locals. He readily joined in local festivities and dances, and he was particularly fond of children, at times interrupting his round of *takuhatsu* in order to join their games. When he came upon other beggars while he was engaged in begging for food, it was not uncommon for him to give what little he had to them.

He spent his days writing poetry in a calligraphy which Alan Watts aptly described as "spidery" but made no particular effort to publish it. He composed in both Japanese and Chinese, and admired the work of the Chinese Zen poets, Kanzan and Jittoku

[Hanshan and Shide, cf. *Zen Masters of China*, Chapter Ten], with whom he would later be compared. He formed friendships with a few contemporary poets who made their way to his isolated hermitage, but beyond this group his own work was not well known. He did not consider himself a professional poet and once remarked that he did not like poetry written by poets nor the calligraphy done by calligraphers.

He resided at Gogoan and later at a second hermitage near the Shinto shrine of Otogo until he was 70, by which time poor health required him to accept the hospitality of a disciple, Kimura Motoemon. It was while staying with Kimura that Ryokan met a Buddhist nun named Teishin. She was in her thirties, but the two became instant companions.

Teishin lived with him for his remaining years. After his death, she went through the nearly 1400 poems he had left behind and began the project of publishing them. The volume she released in 1835 was entitled *Dew Drops on a Lotus Leaf* and was immediately popular.

Because he did not think of himself as a professional poet, Ryokan was not as concerned about the structure of his verse as, for example, Basho had been. Although the poems were recognizable forms, like haiku or waka (five lines of 5, 7, 5, 7, and 7 beats), he did not always strictly adhere to the syllable count.

His subject matter was very commonplace things—children, the physical environment, and the events of his daily life; his poems are infused with a love of nature. He composed love poems to Teishin, and he dealt with traditional Zen topics, as in this pithy summary of Zen practice:

Mind is Buddha
The Way goes nowhere
Look for nothing else
If, to go south, you head north
How will you reach the goal?

Where there is beauty, there is ugliness as well
Where there is right, wrong.
Wisdom and ignorance compliment each other
Illusion and enlightenment cannot be parted.
So it has been since times of old
How could it be otherwise?
To seek one without the other
Is the height of folly.
Even to speak of it in wonder—
All things are impermanent.

This hut on the mountain side
hidden in the trees—
for how many years my home?
At this time of departure,
my thoughts fade like summer verdure.
I meander down the path—
to and fro like the evening star—
the hut, the stand of trees,
no longer visible.
At each turn along the way,
I glance back up the mountain side.

Nothing to offer
but a lotus
floating in a cup of water.

Once again I have forgotten my bowl.
May none pick it up—
my lonely little bowl!

Zen Master Ryokan—
such a simpleton—
body and mind fallen away!

Reflecting on a number of children who had died in a small-
pox epidemic, he wrote:

When spring comes
flowers will blossom
from every branch.
But the children who fell
with the leaves of autumn
will never return.

One evening a thief came upon Ryokan's hermitage, but the Zen Master lived in such poverty that there was nothing for him to take. The disappointed robber was just leaving when Ryokan returned home and found him there.

"It's a shame that you've come all this way and not received anything for your troubles," the poet said, stripping off his robe. "Here. Please take this."

Deeply confused, the thief took the robe and rushed off.

Afterwards, Ryokan sat on the floor, clothed only in his waist-cloth, and enjoyed the moonlight.

The event inspired his best-known haiku:

> The thief left it behind—
> moonlight
> through the window.

Late one afternoon, a visitor from the capital came to see Ryokan. The poet greeted his guest but lamented that he did not have anything suitable to serve him. "I know!" he said. "Please make yourself comfortable here for just a moment, and I'll go into the village to buy some sake for us."

The visitor agreed to his arrangement and settled himself in the small hermitage to wait for Ryokan's return. The visitor amused himself by looking over some of Ryokan's poems, then he noticed that the late afternoon had turned to dusk. Soon it was night, and still Ryokan had not returned. Concerned that something might have happened to his host, the guest set off in the direction of the village. He had not gone very far, however, before he found Ryokan seated at the side of the road gazing into the night sky.

"Master, are you all right?" the visitor asked. "I've been expecting you for several hours now. I was afraid you must have had an accident."

"Please, look," Ryokan told his friend, gesturing to the sky. "Isn't the moon lovely tonight!"

"Yes, I suppose it is. But where's the sake you were getting?"

"The sake? Oh dear, I forgot all about it," Ryokan said getting to his feet. "Please make yourself at home in my hut, and I'll rush to the village right now and get us some."

Ryokan frequently played games with the children of the village. One of their favorites was hide-and-seek. On one occasion, Ryokan hid under a mound of hay. It was a very good hiding place, and the children could not find him. Eventually they tired of the game and returned to their homes. When the farmer, whose hay it was, started to load it upon a cart, he found Ryokan concealed beneath it.

"What are you doing?" the farmer demanded.

"Sshh!" Ryokan whispered. "Don't let the children hear you."

Ryokan ate only what he gathered from his daily round of *takuhatsu* regardless of what it was. One day, a housewife gave him a piece of fish. He was enjoying the fish as he sat on his veranda when a visitor happened by.

"Buddhism prohibits the taking of life," the visitor admonished Ryokan. "It's against the precepts to eat flesh."

"Oh, I don't mind so much," Ryokan said. "I eat fish when it's available, and at other times I let lice and fleas feast on me. It's all the same to me."

Ryokan did not always exhibit what others would consider good common sense. On one occasion, he found a bamboo shoot growing up through the floor of his cottage. He cleared the area around the shoot and nurtured it. Eventually it was a full grown bamboo stalk, and not long after that it reached almost to the roof of the room. Ryokan decided to clear away a section of ceiling for it. He used a candle to burn a hole in the straw, but the whole roof caught fire and the hut—along with the bamboo stalk—was burned to the ground.

One day, a delegation of family members came to express concern about Ryokan's nephew who had fallen into a dissipated life-style. The nephew was the son of Ryokan's brother, Yoshiyuki, and would at some time in the future be expected to inherit his father's responsibilities.

"He won't listen to anything anyone says to him, but he admires you," the spokesman for the group said. "If you came to speak to him, perhaps he would listen to what you have to say."

Ryokan went to the nephew's house, where the young man, who did indeed feel a great deal of affection for his uncle, welcomed him. Instead of lecturing his nephew about his lifestyle, Ryokan spent the evening drinking sake with him and discussing events in general. After a bit, the nephew said he had to retire for the night, and he invited Ryokan to remain there that evening rather than try to make his way back to Gogoan. Ryokan accepted the invitation, and the nephew saw him settle into meditation posture in front of the hearth and enter into zazen.

In the morning, when the nephew awoke, Ryokan was still seated in meditation.

"I must be on my way," Ryokan said, getting to his feet.

He took up his sandals but had some difficulty putting them on. "It's the arthritis in my hands," he explained. "Could you please help me tie them?"

The nephew gladly did so.

Then Ryokan stood in the doorway a moment before leaving. "This is the way of things. Every day, we grow older and more feeble. Please take care of yourself."

The nephew abandoned his former lifestyle as of that morning.

On his deathbed in 1831, Ryokan presented Teishin with his final poem:

> First their fronts
> Then their backs
> Falling maple leaves

After Ryokan's death, his original scrolls and manuscripts became valued treasures, and reproductions of his calligraphy were carved into rocks so that people could make rubbings of them and have their own copies in his distinctive hand.

Portait of Soyen Shaku by Molly Macnaughton

CHAPTER NINETEEN

THE MEIJI ERA

NAN-IN

TANZAN

OGINO DOKUON

IMAKITA KOSEN

SOYEN SHAKU

After the expulsion of foreigners from Japan in the 17th century, the Tokugawa Shogunate instituted an isolationist policy which cut Japan off from the rest of the world. Japanese nationals were not allowed to the leave the islands, and foreigners were not allowed into the country. The only exceptions to this seclusion were associated with trade agreements that Japan maintained with the Dutch and the Chinese.

In 1853, this policy was challenged when US warships sailed into Tokyo Harbor. The Americans, in the person of Commodore Matthew Perry, demanded that the Japanese sign a "Treaty of Peace and Amity" in which they agreed to provide provisions and water to US trading vessels passing through Japanese waters on their way to and from the mainland of Asia; it also required the Japanese to permit the establishment of trade missions from the United States and European nations. Foreigners once more had the right to reside in Japan and own property. The Japanese recognized that these steps were part of the global imperialist efforts of the Western powers, but they did not have the military strength to resist the might of the US navy.

Opponents of the Tokugawa, especially two families from the Southwest—the Satsuma and the Choshu—saw the concessions which Shogun Tokugawa Iemochi had reluctantly made as an insult to Japanese sovereignty and a sign that the Shogunate was no longer effective. They blamed the Tokugawa isolationist policies for the fact that Japan had fallen behind the rest of the world in weaponry and technology, and they maintained that, if the Japanese were to be able to ensure their continued independence, steps needed to be taken to modernize the country. A movement was organized to oust the Shogunate and begin a process of modernizing Japan by taking the counter-intuitive step of returning to direct rule by the current emperor, Osahito (better known by his posthumous name, Komei). Ryokan's father, Tachibana Inan, was one of those who believed a new government headed by the Emperor should be established, and he committed ritual suicide as a sign of his support for that proposal.

Aware that the Satsuma and Choshu were gathering strength, Shogunate forces confronted them in 1866, and then again in 1867. In both instances, the Tokugawa forces were defeated. The combined anti-government forces then easily took control of Edo, and the following January it was announced that the Shogunate was over and that direct rule had been returned to the Tenno—the Heavenly Sovereign. Komei was dead, so command of the new government fell to his fifteen-year-old son, Mutshuhito. The new government was called Meiji (Enlightened Rule), which would become Mutshuhito's posthumous name. The new Emperor left the old capital of Kyoto and established his residence in Edo, now renamed Tokyo.

Many of the young emperor's advisors were neo-Confucionists of the type with whom Suzuki Shosan had contended. Their immediate concern was to develop the technological and military strength of the country in order to be able to resist the interference of foreign powers in Japanese affairs. They recognized that in order to do so they needed to modernize the education system. The easiest way to accomplish that would be by making use of the schools already attached to religious institutions. However, these men also had a deep suspicion about the religion that operated the largest number of these schools.

They perceived Buddhism as a foreign and enervating influence in Japan. They envisioned a nation united by a single religion— Shinto—headed by the Emperor. All Buddhist ceremonies were suspended at the court, and an edict went out demanding that Shinto and Buddhist activities be separated in those temples that served both traditions. Government support for Buddhist temples was suspended, causing financial challenges to many. Early in the regime, there was even an outbreak of popular anger in some regions where the population had come to believe that Buddhist monks led parasitic lives. A number of Soto temples in rural areas were burned, but that degree of animosity was short-lived.

The Buddhist hierarchy responded by trying to demonstrate their loyalty to both the Emperor and the Nation. A group was initiated called the United Movement for Revering the Emperor and Worshipping the Buddha. Reforms were enacted. The Soto leadership recognized that one of their failings had been that they did not have adequate numbers of trained priests to serve in local temples, and as a result too many unqualified individuals had been given responsibilities they were incapable of carrying out, fueling some of the popular anger that manifested itself in the early years of the Meiji Era. They sought to re-establish more effective training techniques by returning to the guidelines established by their founder, Dogen. The *Shobogenzo*, which had fallen into obscurity, was rediscovered and became the basis of Soto teaching and practice. The Rinzai School was better able to weather the challenges of the period because of the extensive reforms that had already been initiated by Hakuin and his followers.

The original inclination of the new government had been to attempt to suppress Buddhism, but the faith was too deeply engrained in the nation for them to be able to accomplish that, so they settled for trying to co-opt it. A Ministry for Religion and Education replaced the short-lived Ministry of Shinto, and it drew up a national education agenda to be carried out by all religious institutions. This was known as the *Daikyo*—or Great Doctrine. It had three major principles.

> Formulated by the government as an expression of the Japanese religious worldview, these principles required (1) respect for the gods (*kami*) and a patriotic devotion to the nation, (2) recognition of "the reason of heaven" and "the way of humanity," and (3) reverence toward the emperor and submission to authority. (57)

A national institute, the Daikyoin, was established to promote the Great Doctrine; its members included Buddhist as well as Shinto and Confucian educators. Changes were made in the traditional curriculum offered at temple schools; now, in addition to philosophy and arts, the schools had to teach mathematics and foreign languages, in particular, English. By 1880, school attendance was made compulsory, and Buddhist schools were actively engaged in supporting the national agenda.

The threat to Buddhism passed, but the Meiji Era remained a challenging one for Buddhists of all schools.

In 1919, shortly after the end of Meiji era, a Zen monk, Nyogen Senzaki—who would later play a major role in introducing Zen to the west—published a small book entitled *101 Zen Stories*. His collection of brief tales included incidents from the life of the Buddha as well as stories about figures from the history of Zen in both China and Japan. Senzaki's selection was intended to provide an introduction to the Zen perspective, and several of the most memorable stories dealt with masters of the Meiji Era. The book was later translated by Senzaki's American student, Paul Reps, and released in English in 1939. Senzaki and Reps collaborated on two smaller books as well, one a translation of the *Mumonkan*. All three works were combined into a single volume, *Zen Flesh, Zen Bones*, which came out in 1957 and quickly became one of the most popular works on Zen in the English language.

The Meiji masters included in the *101 Zen Stories* were not figures of the same stature as Sengai or Ryokan, but the tales associated with them became well known in the west and are frequently quoted.

Nan-in

The opening story is about Nan-in, who has been identified as a Rinzai master in the Hakuin line of descent. The story, however, may have been misattributed to him; Senzaki's scholarship was not always exact. The incident described might actually have been a tale from the Chinese Tang dynasty about a Zen master with a similar name.

> Nan-in, a Japanese master during the Meiji era (1868-1812), received a university professor who came to inquire about Zen.
>
> Nan-in served tea. He poured his visitor's cup full, and then kept on pouring.
>
> The professor watched the overflow until he no longer could restrain himself. "It is overfull. No more will go in!"
>
> "Like this cup," Nan-in said, "you are full of your own opinions and speculations. How can I show you Zen unless you first empty your cup?" (58)

Tanzan

Tanzan was a professor at the western-style Imperial University as well as being an accomplished Zen master. The famous story told about him has even been included in an American picture book for children:

Tanzan and Ekido were once traveling together down a muddy road. A heavy rain was still falling.

Coming around a bend, they met a lovely girl in a silk kimono and sash, unable to cross the intersection.

"Come on, girl," said Tanzan at once. Lifting her in his arms, he carried her over the mud.

Ekido did not speak again until that night when they reached a lodging temple. Then he no longer could restrain himself. "We monks don't go near females," he told Tanzan, "especially not young and lovely ones. It is dangerous. Why did you do that?"

"I left the girl there," said Tanzan. "Are you still carrying her?" (59)

According to another story, Tanzan announced his impending death by sending his disciples post cards on which he wrote: "I'm departing this world. This is my last announcement."

OGINO DOKUON

Ogino Dokuon was recognized as one of the most outspoken opponents of government policies to limit and control Buddhist teaching during the early Meiji Era. He had studied under the demanding Rinzai teacher, Daisetsu Shoen, for fourteen years before his enlightenment was confirmed. He later succeeded Shoen as abbot of Shokokuji.

Yamaoka Tesshu, as a young student of Zen, visited one master after another. He called upon Dokuon of Shokoku.

Desiring to show his attainment, he said: "The mind, Buddha, and sentient beings, after all, do not exist. The true nature of phenomena is emptiness. There is no realization, no delusion, no sage, no mediocrity. There is no giving and nothing to be received."

Dokuon, who was smoking quietly, said nothing. Suddenly he whacked Yamaoka with his bamboo pipe. This made the youth quite angry.

"If nothing exists," inquired Dokuon, "where did this anger come from?" (60)

Imakita Kosen

There are two tales in this collection of 101 stories concerning Nyogen Senzaki's teacher, Soyen Shaku. Shaku was a disciple of Imakita Kosen, possibly the most important Zen figure of the period. Kosen's skill as a calligrapher has already been alluded to in Chapter Ten.

Kosen was born to an upper class Confucian family and, as a child, he was sent to the Confucian school headed by Fujisawa Togai. Togai also introduced his students to the work of Confucius's great Daoist challenger, Laozi. From his reading of Laozi, Kosen developed a desire to better understand the inner experience of Dao and, to that end, applied for admission to the Zen temple, Shokokuji, then under the direction of Daisetsu Shoen. He worked with Shoen for seven years then, at that master's suggestion, continued his training with another teacher at Sogenji. There he finally attained awakening, which he attempted to describe in writing.

One night during zazen practice the boundary between before and after suddenly disappeared. I entered into the blessed realm of the totally wondrous. It was as if I had arrived at the ground of the Great Death, with no memory of the existence of anything, not even myself. All I remember is an energy in my body that spread out over ten times ten-thousand worlds and a light that radiated endlessly. At one point, as I took a breath, seeing and hearing, speaking and moving suddenly became different from what they had normally been. As I sought for the highest principle and the wondrous meaning of the universe, my own self became clear and all things appeared bright. In this abundance of delight, I forgot that my hands were moving in the air and my feet were dancing. (61)

SOYEN SHAKU

There are two "stories" about Soyen Shaku in Senzaki's book, although one is not a narrative but rather a list of rules that Soyen developed for himself and to which he adhered throughout his life:

In the morning before dressing, light incense and meditate.

Retire at a regular hour. Partake of food at regular intervals. Eat with moderation and never to the point of satisfaction.

Receive a guest with the same attitude you have when alone. When alone, maintain the same attitude you have in receiving guests.

Watch what you say, and whatever you say, practice it.

When an opportunity comes do not let it pass by, yet always think twice before acting.

Do not regret the past. Look to the future.

Have the fearless attitude of a hero and the loving heart of a child.

Upon retiring, sleep as if you had entered your last sleep. Upon awakening, leave your bed behind you instantly as if you had cast away a pair of old shoes. (62)

Soyen Shaku was born Tsunejiro Ichinose in 1859. He was sent to a local temple school where, in an autobiographical statement he wrote later, he was taught to respect the Three Treasures (Buddha, Dharma, and Sangha) as well as to be "filial to my parents and helpful to my brother and sisters, to be loyal to my country and faithful to my compatriots." (63)

His older brother, Chutaro, felt drawn to monastic life, but family responsibilities after the death of their father prevented him from doing so. Tsunejiro decided to take the precepts in his brother's stead and became a monk at the age of twelve. He was originally given the Buddhist name Soko. However, because another monk had the same name, their teacher invited Tsunejiro to choose his own name. He elected Soyen in honor of a younger monk of that name who had died.

He studied with two prior masters before he came to work with Kosen at Engakuji, and under their direction was formally introduced to zazen. He was so committed to the practice that during one Rohatsu Sesshin (the December retreat marking the anniversary of the Buddha's enlightenment), he sat outside for two days so wholly absorbed in meditation that he failed to notice when he became covered with snow. Soyen received *inka* from Kosen at the age of 25. At that time, Kosen is said to have remarked that his young disciple was a "born bodhisattva."

Although Kosen fought the restrictions initially placed upon Buddhism by the Meiji regime, he came to be a supporter of the government's policies and even accepted an appointment to serve as an Instructor for the Ministry of Doctrine. He shared the government's belief that it was essential for Japan to adopt those western institutions that could best assist in its modernization. So after Soyen completed his Zen training, rather than having him go on the traditional pilgrimage to Zen temples in the country, Kosen encouraged him to enroll in the new Keio University.

Soyen stayed there for three years, after which he made use of the greater freedom the Japanese now had to travel outside their country to visit Ceylon (now Sri Lanka). His goal was to deepen his understanding of Buddhism by familiarizing himself with the older Theravada tradition, but the young Japanese found conditions in the island nation extremely difficult. He wrote back to Kosen that the only thing in Ceylon that seemed the same as at home was the barking of the dogs. In particular, he was unprepared for the tropical heat which was so severe he was unable to take part in the traditional begging rounds with the other monks.

He admired the life-style of the Ceylonese monks—*bhikkus*—and their commitment to the precepts; however, he was never able to communicate with them very well, and he realized that they would be bewildered if he attempted to explain Zen with its emphasis on personal enlightenment.

In a talk given to his American students in 1947, Nyogen Senzaki told this story about Soyen's return trip to Japan after spending three years in Ceylon. He went from Singapore to Thailand on a steamship. He had almost no money and could only afford to travel as a deck passenger. He was still unused to the tropical heat, and the glare of the sun on the open deck of the ship was a misery.

There was little water, and he had no food. Then, to make his situation even worse, the ship had to anchor on the coast at the mouth of a river in order to wait for the turn of the tide. The deck passengers were immediately attacked by hordes of mosquitoes. As evening approached, dark clouds appeared in the distance that only made the humidity more oppressive, and he could get no rest because of the heat and the voracious pests. Finally, he found a small area on the deck that provided him a little privacy. There he removed most of his clothing and formed it into a cushion to sit upon, then tried to enter meditation—allowing the mosquitoes to feed as much as they liked on his bare skin. For a long while the drone of the feeding insects prevented him from entering into the state of samadhi, but eventually he succeeded and his mind became fully concentrated. He was no longer aware of the mosquitoes, the heat, or his thirst. When a rainstorm roused him from his meditation, he heard in the distance a temple bell ringing, and he smiled in contentment. Looking about he saw that a number of bright red wild berries of some kind had fallen about him. Examining them more closely, he discovered they were not berries at all, but mosquitoes so engorged with his blood that they were unable to fly.

A year after Soyen returned to Japan, Kosen died, and his young disciple was appointed principal teacher at Engakuji.

As had Kosen, Soyen supported the policies of the Meiji government, including their military excursions into China and Russia. During the Russo-Japanese War [1904-05], he took time from his duties at Engakuji to serve as a chaplain in the First Army Division and would later argue that the Japanese victory was due, in part, to the strength the nation drew from Buddhist culture and specifically from Zen training which aided in instilling a "samurai spirit" in the population. It was a point of view in which many people in the higher levels of government began to see some validity. By the end of the Russo-Japanese War, Zen practice was no longer considered suspect.

The Meiji Era came to an end with the death of the Emperor in 1912. The period lasted less than forty-five years, a relatively short time in history. However the changes that were wrought in Japan during those years were brisk and effective. By the end of the Meiji Era, Japan was recognized as a world power on a par with the United States and the more developed nations of Europe. Japan was now a major player on the global stage, and the scene was set for Zen to move beyond the confines of Asia.

Epilogue in Chicago

By the end of the 19th Century, Asian studies had not only acquired a degree of respectability in the West, they had also attracted a popular interest that would not have been imaginable only a few decades earlier. But then the post-Darwinian world was a place of rapid change.

While Christian doctrine was under attack from scientific rationalism, a group of scholars and translators wondered if non-theistic Buddhism—especially as expressed in the Theravada tradition—might not provide the basis for a faith system better suited to bridge the growing rift between science and religion. In popular culture, charlatans like the Russian-born founder of Theosophy—Helena Petrovna Blavatsky—made claims about the mysterious doctrines of the East that found willing adherents among the gullible and desperate.

Liberal Christians sought for a means of regaining lost ground and establishing a rapprochement with the scientific community. They chose the Chicago World's Fair of 1893 as their venue. Also known as the Columbian Exposition, the Fair marked the 400th anniversary of Columbus's first voyage to the Americas and was touted to be a celebration of Western technological achievement. A World Parliament of Religions was proposed which would take place at the same time. It was to be a gathering of representatives from the major religious traditions of the globe. The organizers hoped to be able to identify principles shared by all faiths and then, no doubt, to demonstrate that Christianity provided the most fully evolved exposition of those principles.

Among those invited to participate in the Parliament was the Japanese Zen Abbot, Soyen Shaku. Some of his colleagues advised him to refuse the invitation on the grounds that the barbarians of the United States would not be able to understand or appreciate the Buddha Dharma; however, after giving the invitation careful consideration, Soyen decided to take part. He composed a paper on the Buddhist teachings regarding cause and effect, and, because he did not know English, he asked one his students to translate it into that language for him. The student was Teitaro Suzuki, whose Buddhist name—Daisetsu—meant "Great Humility."

Soyen was in Chicago for the presentation of his paper, which was read on his behalf by one of the Parliament's organizers. In the audience at the time was a German Orientalist resident in nearby LaSalle, Illinois, Paul Carus. Carus approached Soyen and asked if he would consider assisting him in a project to make translations of Buddhist writings available in the West. Soyen demurred, explaining that he was not qualified to do so nor could he take further time from his duties at Engakuji. He did, however, suggest that the young student who had translated his paper into English might be up to the task.

So it was that D. T. Suzuki came to Illinois in 1897, and—with him—Zen took its third step east, across the Pacific Ocean, to the Americas.

Acknowledgments

The author gratefully acknowledges permission to reprint the following material:

- Hackett Publishing Company for excerpts from: Stephen Addiss, Stanley Lombardo and Judith Roitman (eds.), *Zen Sourcebook* (2008.)

- Excerpts from *Zen Buddhism: A History—Japan* by Heinrich Dumoulin © World Wisdom, Inc, 2005. All selections used with permission.

- The Rochester Zen Center for their translation of *Master Hakuin's Chant in Praise of Zazen.*

- Tuttle Publishing for excepts from *Zen Flesh, Zen Bones* by Paul Reps and Nyogen Senzaki, and *An Introduction to Zen Training* by Omori Sogen

- Michael Gamer, Anne Watts, and Joan Watts for excerpts from: *Zen Dust* by Isshu Miura and Ruth Sasaki.

- Excerpts from *Essays in Zen Buddhism*, copyright © by D. T. Suzuki. Used by permission of Grove/Atlantic, Inc. Any third party use of this material, outside of this publication, is prohibited.

- Seven lines by Keizin Jokin from *The Light Inside the Dark* by John Tarrant. Copyright © 1998 by John Tarrant. Reprinted by permission of HarperCollins Publishers.

- Ikkyu, excepts from *Crow With No Mouth*, versions by Stephen Berg. Copyright © 1989, 2000 by Stephen Berg. Reprinted with the permission of The Permissions Company, Inc., on behalf of Copper Canyon Press, www.coppercanyonpress.org.

Notes

1. Richard Bryan McDaniel, *Zen Masters of China: The First Step East* (Rutland, VT: Charles E. Tuttle Co., Inc., 2012), pp. 15-16

2. D. T. Suzuki, *Essays in Zen Buddhism, First Series* (London: Rider and Company, 1973), pp. 196-97.

3. Peter Mathiessen, *Nine-Headed Dragon River* (Boston: Shambala, 1998), p. 155.

4. Heinrich Dumoulin, *Zen Buddhism: A History – Japan* (Bloomington, IN: World Wisdom, 2005), p. 22.

5. Mathiessen, op. cit., p. 169.

6. Francis Dojun Cook, *How to Raise an Ox* (Boston: Wisdom Publications, 2002), pp. 65-66.

7. Ibid., p. 66.

8. Thomas Cleary (trans.), *Shobogenzo: Zen Essays by Dogen* (Honolulu: University of Hawaii Press, 1986), pp. 32-34.

9. Dumoulin, op. cit, p. 124.

10. The illustration introducing Chapter Twenty-One of *Zen Masters of China* is a portrait of Mujun Shiban.

11. Suzuki, op. cit., p. 256.

12. Ibid., p. 257.

13. Paul Reps, *Zen Flesh, Zen Bones* (Garden City, NY: Anchor Books, no date), p. 31.

14. Dumoulin, op. cit., p. 27.

15. Isshu Miura and Ruth Fuller Sasaki, *Zen Dust* (New York: Harcourt, Brace & World), p. 201.

16. Dumoulin, op. cit., p. 39.

17. Miura and Sasaki, op. cit., p. 206.

18. Dumoulin, op. cit., p. 186.

19. Ibid., p. 188.

20. Miura and Sasaki, op. cit., p. 234.

21. Ibid., p. 325.

22. Dumoulin, op. cit., p. 140.

23. John Tarrant, *The Light Inside the Dark* (New York, Harper, 1998), p. 210.

24. Dumoulin, op. cit., p. 157.

25. Ibid., pp. 167-68.

26. Reps, op. cit., pp. 78-79.

27. Dumoulin, op. cit., pp. 199-200.

28. Ibid., p. 194.

29. Stephen Berg, *Crow with No Mouth* (Port Townsend, WA: Copper Canyon Press, 2000), p. 58.

30. Stephen Addiss, et. al. (ed), *Zen Sourcebook* (Indianapolis: Hackett Publishing Company, 2008), p. 202.

31. Ibid., p. 204.

32. Berg, op. cit., p. 66.

33. Omori Sogen, *An Introduction to Zen Training* (Rutland, VT: Tuttle Publishing, 2001), p. 97.

34. Berg, op. cit, p. 75.

35. See the illustration introducing Chapter Five of *Zen Masters of China*.

36. Dumoulin, op. cit., p. 237.

37. D. T. Suzuki, *Zen and Japanese Culture* (Princeton: Bollingen, 1973), p. 295.

38. Dumoulin, op. cit., p. 277.

39. Suzuki, op. cit., pp. 95-96.

40. Ibid., p. 100.

41. Arthur Braverman, *Warrior of Zen* (New York: Kodansha International, 1994), p. 36.

42. See the illustrations introducing Chapters Eleven through Twenty of *Zen Masters of China*.

43. Braverman, op. cit., p. 47.

44. Dumoulin, op. cit., p. 330.

45. Norman Waddell (ed., and trans.), *The Unborn: The Life and Teachings of Zen Master Bankei* (New York: North Point Press, 2000), pp. 136.

46. Ibid., pp. 40-41.

47. Makoto Ueda, *Matsuo Basho* (New York: Kodansha International, 1982), p. 126.

48. Ibid., p. 132.

49. Thomas Cleary, *Zen Antics* (Boston: Shambhala, 1993), p. 88.

50. Miura and Sasaki, op. cit., pp. 46-47.

51. *Chants and Recitations* (Rochester: Rochester Zen Center, 2005), pp. 34-35.

52. Thomas Cleary (trans.), *The Undying Lamp of Zen* (Boston: Shambala, 2011), p. 78.

53. *Chants and Recitations*, p. 36.

54. Cleary, *Zen Antics*, p. 68.

55. Taizan Maezumi and Bernie Glassman, *On Zen Practice* (Boston: Wisdom Publications, 2002), p. 84.

56. Dumoulin, op. cit., p. 345.

57. Ibid., p. 402.

58. Reps, op. cit., p. 5.

59. Ibid., p. 18.

60. Ibid., pp. 69-70.

61. Dumoulin, op. cit., p. 408.

62. Reps, op. cit. p. 26.

63. Nyogen Senzaki, *Eloquent Silence* (ed. Sherry Chayat), (Boston: Wisdom Publications, 2008), p. 351.

Bibliography

Addiss, Stephen and Stanley Lombardo and Judith Roitman (eds.). *Zen Sourcebook*. Indianapolis: Hackett Publishing Company, 2008.

Aitkin, Robert. *Taking the Path of Zen*. New York: North Point Press, 1982.

Berg, Stephen (trans.). *Crow with No Mouth*. Port Townsend, WA: Copper Canyon Press, 2000.

Braverman, Arthur (ed. and trans.). *Warrior of Zen*. New York: Kodansha International, 1994.

Cleary, Thomas [trans.]. *Shobogenzo: Zen Essays by Dogen*. Honolulu: University of Hawaii Press, 1992.

Cleary, Thomas. *Timeless Spring*. Rutland, VT: Tuttle Publishing, 1980.

Cleary, Thomas. *The Undying Lamp of Zen*. Boston: Shambhala, 2011.

Cleary, Thomas [trans. and edit]. *Zen Antics*, Boston: Shambhala, 1993.

Cook, Francis Dojun. *How to Raise an Ox*. Boston: Wisdom Publications, 2002.

Dumoulin, Heinrich. *Zen Buddhism: A History - India and China*. Bloomington, IN: World Wisdom, 1988.

Dumoulin, Heinrich. *Zen Buddhism: A History – Japan*. Bloomington, IN: World Wisdom, 1990.

Durant, Will. *Our Oriental Heritage*. New York: MJF Books, 1993.

Ferguson, Andy. *Zen's Chinese Heritage*. Boston: Wisdom Publications, 2000.

Furuta, Shokin. *Sengai: Master Zen Painter*. New York: Kodansha International, 2000.

Hoover, Thomas. *The Zen Experience*. New York: New American Library, 1980.

Kraft, Kenneth (ed). *Zen Teaching, Zen Practice*. Boston: Weatherhill, 2000.

Kraft, Kenneth (ed.). *Zen: Tradition and Transition*. New York: Grove/Atlantic, 1988.

Low, Albert. *Hakuin on Kensho*. Boston: Shambhala, 2006.

Low, Albert. *Zen Meditation Plain and Simple*. Rutland, VT: Tuttle Publishing, 2000.

Matthiessen, Peter. *Nine-Headed Dragon River*. Boston: Shambala, 1998.

McDaniel, Richard Bryan. *Zen Masters of China: The First Step East*. Rutland, VT: Tuttle Publishing, 2012.

Miura, Isshu and Ruth Sasaki. *Zen Dust*. New York: Harcourt, Brace and World, 1966.

Nukariya, Kaiten. *The Religion of the Samurai*. New York: Taylor and Francis, 2005.

Omori Sogen. *An Introduction to Zen Training*. Rutland, VT: Tuttle Publishing, 2001.

Reps, Paul and Nyogen Senzaki. *Zen Flesh, Zen Bones*. Rutland, VT: Tuttle Publishing, 1998.

Rochester Zen Center. *Chants and Recitations*. Rochester: Rochester Zen Center, 2005.

Ryokan. *One Robe, One Bowl: The Zen Poetry of Ryokan*. Boston: Weatherhill, 2006.

Sekida, Katsuki. *Two Zen Classics*. Boston: Shambhala, 2005.

Senzaki, Nyogen. *Eloquent Silence*. Boston: Wisdom Publications, 2008.

Shodo Harada. *The Path to BodhiDharma*. Rutland, Vermont: Tuttle Publishing, 2000.

Snyder, Gary. *Riprap and Cold Mountain Poems*. Berkeley: Counterpoint, 2010.

Suzuki, D. T. *Essays in Zen Buddhism, First Series*. New York: Grove Press, 1994.

Suzuki, D. T. *Essays in Zen Buddhism, Third Series*. Newburyport, MA: Samuel Weiser, 1971.

Suzuki, D. T. *Sengai: The Zen of Ink and Paper*. Boston: Shambhala, 1999.

Suzuki, D. T. *Zen and Japanese Culture*. Princeton: Princeton University Press, 2010.

Suzuki, D. T. *The Zen Doctrine of No-Mind*. Newburyport, MA: Samuel Weiser, 1991.

Tames, Richard. *A Traveller's History of Japan*. New York: Interlink Books, 2008.

Ueda, Makoto. *The Master Haiku Poet Matsuo Basho*. Tokyo: Kodansha International, 1982.

Victoria, Brian Daizen. *Zen at War*. Oxford: Rowman and Littlefield, 2006.

Waddell, Norman. *The Unborn: The Life and Teachings of Zen Master Bankei*. New York: North Point Press, 1984.

Watts, Alan. *The Way of Zen*. New York: Vintage, 1999.

Index of Stories

Bankei Yotaku, 194-208
  "What is inherent
    nature?", 196
  And Umpo Zenjo, 197
  Initial awakening, 198
  And Dosha Chogen, 199
  Full awakening, 200
  The Unborn Buddha
    mind, 203
  "Image a woman sewing",
    204
  A rival priest, 204
  Magic is not the way of
    Zen, 205
  The thief monk, 205
  A man with a violent
    temper, 206
  The Tendai monk, 206
  The sleeping monk, 207
  Futility of trying to rid the
    mind of thoughts, 207
  Futility of looking for a
    technique, 208
  Death, 208
Basho [see Matsuo Basho]
Bassui, 114-125
  Questions about his
    father's death, 116
  "Who is the Master?", 117

And Tokukei Jisha, 120
  Initial kensho, 121
  And Koho Kakumyo, 121
  Letter to a dying man, 124
  Death, 125
Bodhidharma (the First
  Patriarch), 17-22
  And Emperor Wu, 18
  And the Second Patriarch,
    20
  Cut off his eyelids, 39
Bucchi Kakuan, 63
Bukko Kokushi, 74-77
  And Mujun Shiban, 74
  Awakening, 74
  And Mongul soldiers, 75
  And Tokimune, 76

Chiyono, 77-79
  As a servant, 77
  Awakening, 78

Daikin Kokushi [see Mukan
  Fumon]
Dainichi Nonin, 62
Daito Kokushi [see Shuho
  Myocho]
Dogen Kigen, 45-58
  Mother's death, 46

"Why did the masters of old make such efforts?", 47
And Myoan Eisai, 47
And Ryonen Myozen, 48
First tenzo, 48
Second tenzo, 50
And Tendo Nyojo, 50
Awakening, 51
Fukanzazengi, 53
And Koun Ejo, 54
Shobogenzo, 54
"Just one mistake after another", 58
First meeting with Kuon Ejo, 64
And Genmyo, 102
Dokutan Shokei, 192-93
Dokyo Etan, 226-28
Awakening, 226
And Shido Munan, 226
Death poem, 228
And Hakuin Ekaku, 232
Doshin (the Fourth Patriarch), 24-25
Dosha Chogen, 190
And Bankei Yotaku, 199
Dosho, 25

Eka (Ji; the Second Patriarch), 20-24
Enni Ben'en, 79-82
Teaching, 80
Death, 82

Gasan Jito, 260-62

Gien, 70-71
Gudo Toshoku, 184-85
What happens to an enlightened man after death?, 184
"Knocking at the gates of Zen, 185
And Shido Munan, 186
Gyoki, 31

Hakuin Ekaku, 229-250
Fear of Hell, 229
Initial awakening, 232
And Shoju Rojin, 233
Full awakening, 234
Hakuyushi and Zen sickness, 238
Lost reputation, 240
A rough sea crossing, 241
A miser, 242
"A Buddha's ass deserves only the best", 243
"Eat and experience the misery of the common people", 243
"The light of Buddha shines through everything", 244
Death, 245
The sound of one hand, 246
Sermon, 247
Chant in Praise of Zazen, 248
And Torei Enji, 254
And Gasan Jito, 261

Honen, 35
Huike [see Eka]

Ikkyu Sojun, 128-40
  A broken tea cup, 128
  And Kaso Sodon, 129
  Awakening, 131
  Tries to burn his certificate of *inka*, 132
  On spending ten days as a temple administrator, 133
  Koan about the widow, the old monk, and the girl, 134
  A stingy land-owner, 135
  Contest with the Yamabushi monk, 135
  Sample poems, 136-37
  Attention, attention, attention, 139
  Death poem, 140
Imakita Kosen, 294-95
  Calligraphy, 146
Ingen Ryuki, 190-92
Inzan Ien, 262-64

Joshu Jushin
  "Have you had anything to eat?", 9
  "The cypress tree in the garden.", 38
  "Does a dog have Buddha-nature?", 38
Joso, 221-22

Kakua, 28
Kanzan Egen, 97-99
  Kanzan's *inka*, 98
  At Myoshinji, 98
  Death, 99
  And Muso Soseki, 113
Keizan Jokin, 102-07
  Mother's devotion to Kannon, 102
  Awakening, 104
  Zazen Yojinki, 104
Kobo Daishi, 34
Koun Ejo, 63-67
  And Dogen, 54
  Mother's challenge, 63
  First meeting with Dogen, 64
  Awakening, 65
Kukai [see Kobo Daishi]

Matsuo Basho, 212-21
  And Todo Yoshitada, 212
  Zen training and awakening, 214
  Travels, 215
  "I saw something more beautiful than flowers", 218
  Sample haiku, 220
Mugai Nyodai [see Chiyono]
Mukan Fumon, 82-83
  Expels ghosts from the Emperor's palace, 83
Muso Soseki, 107-13
  Dream of Sozan Konin and Sekito Kisen, 108

Awakening, 109
On Mindfulness, 111
Gardens, 112
And Kanzan Egen, 113
Sermon, 113
Murata Shuko, 149-51
Myoan Eisai, 36-42
And Kian Esho, 37
And tea, 39
"Would the Buddha object to giving up his halo?", 41
And Dogen, 47

Nampo Jomyo, 85-87
And Kido Chigu, 85
Death, 86
And Shoho Myocho, 92
Nan-in, 292

Ogino Dokuan, 293-94

Ryokan Daigu, 276-85
Certificate of *inka*, 277
Sample poems, 279
A thief, 281
A visitor from the capital, 281
A game of hide-and-seek, 282
"I eat fish; lice and fleas feast on me," 282
A bamboo shoot, 283
A dissipated nephew, 283
Death poem, 284
Ryonen Myozen, 42-43

And Myoan Eisai, 42
Decision to go to China, 42
And Dogen, 43

Saicho, 40
Sengai Gibon, 268-76
And Gessen Zenne, 268
Enlightenment poem, 269
Retirement to Kyohakuin and art, 270
A monk who snuck out of the monastery, 272
And Tangen Toi, 273
No greater example of good fortune, 274
A daimyo's chrysanthemums, 274
Death, 275
Sessho Toyo, 147-49
A painting of a rat, 147
"Boat of Snow", 148
To save a painting, 149
Shido Munan, 186-89
And Dokyo Etan, 226
Shinchi Kakushin, 83-85
And Mumon Ekai, 84
And Emperor Go-Uta, 84
And Yoritake Ryoen, 85
Shinran, 35
Shoichi Kokushi [see Enni Ben'en]
Shoju Rojim [see Dokyo Etan]
Shotoku (Prince), 30
Shuho Myocho, 90-96

A Zen master living
among beggars, 91
And Nampo Jomyo, 92
And Emperor Hanazono,
94
Teaching, 95
Death, 96
Soeki Rikyu, 151-54
Leaves in the courtyard,
151
And the samurai assassin,
152
A single morning glory,
153
False *sabi*, 153
Death, 154
Soyen Shaku, 295-299
Life rules, 295
Travels to Ceylon, 297
Wild Berries, 297
Invited to the World
Parliament of Religions,
302
Sosan Kanchi (the Third
Patriarch), 22-24
Suzuki Shosan, 170-80
Early preoccupation with
death, 170
Nio statues, 170
Awakening, 172
"Keep death alone in your
heart", 175
"A samurai is more suited
to religious practice than
a monk.", 175

The funeral of a young
man, 175
"Not one person who
lived a hundred years ago
is alive today.", 176
The bird hunter, 176
A group of farmers, 177
Monk Jihon, 177
On the *nembutsu*, 178
Dancing zazen, 178
Death, 180

Takuan Soho, 160-67
The naked monk, 161
"Mystery of Prajna
Immoveable", 165
Takuju Kosen, 264-65
Tanzan, 292-93
Tettsu Gikai, 67-70
Torei Enji, 254-60
And Hakuin, 254
*Discourse on the Inexhaust-
ible Lamp of Zen*, 256
Special powers, 259

Umpo Zenjo, 197

Zhaozhou Congshen [see
Joshu Jushin]

The Tuttle Story: "Books to Span the East and West"

Many people are surprised when they learn that the world's largest publisher of books on Asia had its humble beginnings in the tiny American state of Vermont. The company's founder, Charles Tuttle, came from a New England family steeped in publishing.

Tuttle's father was a noted antiquarian dealer in Rutland, Vermont. Young Charles honed his knowledge of the trade working in the family bookstore, and later in the rare books section of Columbia University Library. His passion for beautiful books—old and new—never wavered throughout his long career as a bookseller and publisher.

After graduating from Harvard, Tuttle enlisted in the military and in 1945 was sent to Tokyo to work on General Douglas MacArthur's staff. He was tasked with helping to revive the Japanese publishing industry, which had been utterly devastated by the war. After his tour of duty was completed, he left the military, married a talented and beautiful singer, Reiko Chiba, and in 1948 began several successful business ventures.

To his astonishment, Tuttle discovered that postwar Tokyo was actually a book-lover's paradise. He befriended dealers in the Kanda district and began supplying rare Japanese editions to American libraries. He also imported American books to sell to the thousands of GIs stationed in Japan. By 1949, Tuttle's business was thriving, and he opened Tokyo's very first English-language bookstore in the Takashimaya Department Store in Ginza, to great success. Two years later, he began publishing books to fulfill the growing interest of foreigners in all things Asian.

Though a westerner, Tuttle was hugely instrumental in bringing a knowledge of Japan and Asia to a world hungry for information about the East. By the time of his death in 1993, he had published over 6,000 books on Asian culture, history and art—a legacy honored by Emperor Hirohito in 1983 with the "Order of the Sacred Treasure," the highest honor Japan can bestow upon a non-Japanese.

The Tuttle company today maintains an active backlist of some 1,500 titles, many of which have been continuously in print since the 1950s and 1960s—a great testament to Charles Tuttle's skill as a publisher. More than 60 years after its founding, Tuttle Publishing is more active today than at any time in its history, still inspired by Charles Tuttle's core mission—to publish fine books to span the East and West and provide a greater understanding of each.

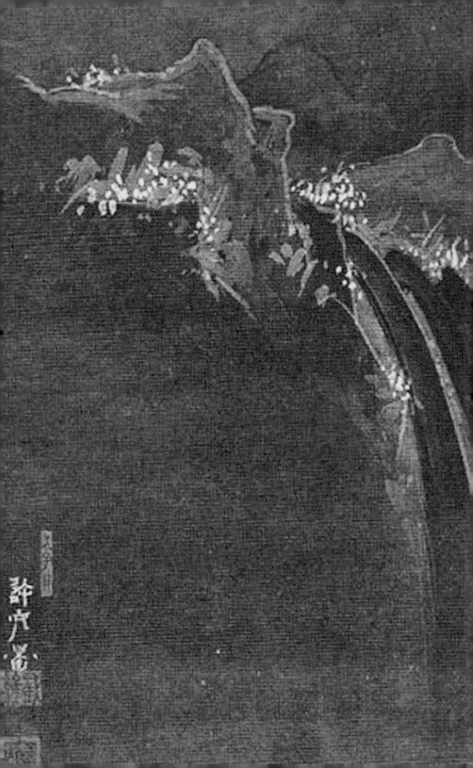